# Buses and Coaches

1945-1965

by

John C. Gillham

ALMARK

Almark Publishing Co. Ltd, London

The illustrations on the front cover are as follows:

*Top left* A Bristol L6B long-distance coach in the Royal Blue fleet of the Southern National Omnibus Co. Ltd of Exeter, parked in 1957 on the edge of Maidenhead coach station.

*Bottom left* A Guy Arab Mark 4 double-decker of the Lancashire United Transport Ltd, with Northern Counties bodywork, dating from 1954, seen at Bolton in 1957.

*Top right* A Dennis Lance K3 double-decker of 1950, with East Lancashire bodywork, owned by the Aldershot & District Traction Co. Ltd, standing in Guildford bus station in 1958.

*Bottom right* A Daimler CVD6 single-decker of 1948 with Alexander bodywork, owned by Aberdeen Corporation Transport, standing in 1958 at the Bridge of Don terminus.



First Published 1976.

ISBN 0 85524 270 1

Printed in Great Britain by
Chapel River Press,
Andover, Hants.
for the publishers, Almark Publishing Co. Ltd,
49 Malden Way, New Malden,
Surrey KT3 6EA, England.

# Preface

Today most double-deck buses have the engines at the rear, and most single-deckers have it under the floor amidships. But this is a recent development. Bus design evolved rapidly from 1900 to 1930, and was then fairly static until 1950. During this period the engine was always at the front, with a prominently visible radiator. The driver either sat behind the engine, with a double-sided bonnet (known as the normal-control layout), or alongside of it with forward control, which usually involved a half-width cab and a half-width bonnet but sometimes a full-width cab completely surrounding the engine. The body was always separate from the chassis, held onto it by only a dozen or so bolts, and often removed again at a major overhaul.

This book describes the big changes of design and layout that were made in the 1950s. The few buses that were built in World War II were all to well-tried orthodox designs, and for a few years afterwards the demand was so heavy that improved versions of these could sell almost faster than makers could produce them. But then masses of bus passengers started buying their own private cars, so the demand for bus and coach services fell. Large increases in the cost of fuel and of crew wages made it desirable to carry more people per bus, and to put the entrance right at the front so that the driver could collect fares from passengers on single-deckers and eliminate the separate conductor, or at least relieve the conductor of the responsibility of the entrance and exit on double-deckers. Changes in the law for single-deckers, around 1950, allowed this to be done.

The overall length and width of buses and coaches (and many other dimensions as well) have always been closely restricted by law, since 1931 by the Construction and Use Regulations of the Ministry of Transport, and the P.S.V. Equipment and Use Regulations. The maximum legal width was increased in 1928 from 7 ft. 2 in. to 7 ft. 6 in, but all through the war some 81 buses well in excess of this were used very successfully in certain parts of Britain. They had been made in 1939-40 for overseas use, but lack of shipping prevented them from being exported. This led to strong pressure from British operators for an 8 ft. width to be allowed for all British buses. This width was authorised as from 1 July 1946, at first on specified routes only. Most operators welcomed this, and bought only wide buses from then onwards. But others still preferred 7 ft. 6 in., and hence for ten years or more most manufacturers made both widths. In autumn 1961 the legal maximum was increased to 8 ft. 2½ in.

On 1 June 1950 the maximum legal length of single-deckers was increased from 27 ft. 6 in. to 30 ft., and of double-deckers from 26 ft. to 27 ft. This meant that instead of 33 seats (or 37 at a squeeze if the engine was a short one) single-deckers could now have 41 seats, and double-deckers could have 64 instead of 56. Most manufacturers at once started making elongated versions of their existing front-engined designs. But by mounting the engine under the floor, and horizontally instead of vertically, extra space could be gained at the front end. In 1949-52, following the lead given by B.M.M.O. in 1946, underfloor-engined single-deck chassis were put into commercial production by Sentinel, A.E.C., Leyland, Guy, Atkinson, Daimler, Bristol, and Dennis, in that sequence, also by six other firms a few years later. The legal maximum length for single-deckers was further increased to 36 ft. in 1961 and to 39 ft. 4 in. in 1968. For double-deckers it was increased to 30 ft. on 1 July 1956, and to 36 ft. in 1961. Underfloor engines were not possible for double-deckers, as the floor had to be kept fairly low to avoid exceeding the legal maximum height of 15 ft. To avoid fouling railway bridges and overhanging trees it was desirable to get a lot lower than this. Very low floor heights, involving some very ingenious and complicated chassis layouts, were introduced by Bristol in 1951 and by A.E.C., Dennis, Guy, and Albion in 1956-61.

Rear engines as a commercial proposition (excluding experimental prototypes) were introduced for single-deckers by Foden in 1950. For double-deckers they did not appear until 1956 (Leyland) and 1960 (Daimler), but these two and the Bristol of 1968 are now the only British double-deckers still being made. Chassisless or integral construction for single-deckers was introduced by Sentinel, Beadle, B.M.M.O., Leyland, Harrington, and A.E.C.

in 1947-53, and for double-deckers by A.E.C. and Guy in 1956-9, but none of them proved as popular as expected, and all vanished after a few years. All makers, of all types of chassis from the largest to the smallest, were constantly striving to reduce weight by using lighter materials. But with more and more private cars coming on the road, hence less demand for new buses and coaches, and increased costs of production, most of the bus chassis makers of the 1950s have now vanished. Twelve were absorbed by others, five now make only lorries, and six just faded away, leaving only six still with us today.

Wheelbase lengths are quoted in this book as they are rather important and are related to overall lengths and turning circles. From 1932 until 1950 the official regulations stipulated that a bus must be able to turn in a circle of 60 ft. dia. if up to 26 ft. long, or 66 ft. dia. if over 26 ft. From 1 June 1950, when longer buses were allowed, the length of 27 ft. was substituted for 26 ft. for both these diameters. From 1 April 1959 the turning circle was measured at the extreme length and width, i.e. the four corners of the overhang, instead of the wheel track, and it had to be not more than 65 ft. dia. for vehicles up to 27 ft. long, or 71 ft. dia. for those over 27 ft. These changes were the cause of many of the alterations to wheelbases referred to in this book.

Bodywork is mentioned only where it was made by the chassis maker himself, or by a specific bodybuilder in close association with the chassis builder. With most makes of chassis a wide variety of different bodies could be fitted. Trolleybuses and minibuses have not been included in this book. We do not overlook the importance of the clutch, gearbox, rear axle, steering, and braking systems, but due to space shortage they are mentioned only where they had some unusual technical features or were the pioneers of a new design.

Engines are described and tabulated separately, because many chassis makers fitted only the units made by one of the specialised engine makers, or by other chassis makers, and did not make their own engines. The largest specialised maker was (and still is) Norris Henty & Gardners Ltd of Paticroft, near Manchester. Their world-famous Gardner LW oil engine range was introduced in 1931 and at once proved so highly successful that since then many thousands have been made for heavy lorry and bus work, with hardly any modifications to the original design. The 4LW, 5LW, 6LW, and 8LW all have the same bore and stroke and main features, differing only in the number of cylinders and in the crankshaft and its bearings. In 1950 the same engines were turned on their sides with new crankcases to make the horizontal HLW range. The smaller LK series was introduced in 1938, and the larger and more powerful LX series in 1958.

Starting in a very small way at Peterborough in 1933 Frank Perkins pioneered the smaller type of oil engine for medium-size and smaller chassis. His engines proved so economical to run that after the war they were in widespread demand for replacing petrol engines in existing chassis, as well as for many makes of new vehicle, both passenger and goods. Soon F. Perkins Ltd had a range of eight basic engine sizes, with variations as required. Henry Meadows Ltd of Wolverhampton were old-established makers of gearboxes and petrol engines before introducing their three basic oil engines, each of which could have either four or six cylinders. Their peculiarity is that the bore and the stroke were the same as each other in each case. A newcomer to Britain in 1963, from America where they were already an enormous organisation, was the Cummins Engine Co. Ltd. They opened a factory at Darlington, and their oil engines were soon adopted for Daimler buses and several British lorry makes. Air-cooled oil engines by Deutz of Germany, and Ruston & Hornsby of Lincoln, were also used in a few British buses in the sixties.

All the black-and-white photographs in this book are from my own camera, except the Jensen, Kew Dodge, and underfloor Seddon, which are by G. R. Mills of Colchester. As far as possible they are all nearside views, as this shows the bonnet and entrance much better. For all the colour photographs, in the book and on the cover, I am grateful to A. P. Tatt of Plumstead. For much of the technical and statistical information I am indebted to all the manufacturers who have allowed me to scrounge and file their sales brochures at every Commercial Motor Show at Earls Court since my schooldays, and to the weekly and monthly technical press which has always been very valuable.

# A.E.C.

*(Southall, Middlesex)*

On 5 November 1945 the last of 9619 "Matador" army lorries came off the Southall assembly line, and was followed immediately by the first post-war bus, a "Regent 0661/20", which went to Mansfield, the first "Regal 0662/20" following two months later. For the time being A.E.C. carried on with its pre-war models, basically the 1933 designs. The Regent and Regal seated up to 56 and 37, with a wheelbase of 16 ft. 3 in. and 17 ft. 6 in., and an overall length of 26 ft. and 27 ft. 6 in. By the time production ceased at the end of 1947 a total of 8,095 and 5,667 had been made since 1929. Both used the famous 7.7-litre oil engine of 1934, of which over 25,000 had already been made and were also used in several other makes of bus and lorry. Both types (post-war) had a friction clutch and clash gearbox instead of the pre-war fluid flywheel and Wilson gearbox. They were used by numerous operators in all parts of Britain, the Regents mainly by municipalities and the Regals mainly by British Electric Traction Co. Ltd subsidiary companies.

The new 9.6-litre direct injection oil engine appeared in March 1946 (although 152 had been made in 1939). This was much bigger and more powerful than any previous bus engine, either of A.E.C. or any other maker. It had high power coupled with lively acceleration for keeping high schedule speeds, whilst its sustained torque at low speeds enabled a heavily-laden vehicle to remain in top gear over varying road and traffic conditions, giving economy in fuel consumption, less wear and tear of the transmission, and the minimum of exertion to the driver. In the 30 years since 1946 it has been a highly successful engine, and widely used in vast quantities in many different applications.

The "Regent Mark III" 56-seat double-decker used this 9.6-litre engine in an entirely new chassis with 16 ft. 4 in. wheelbase, an improved fluid flywheel, and a compressed air-operated Wilson pre-selective epicyclic gearbox. Air brakes were fitted three years before any other chassis maker did so. Some with a low front dash and a new short and wide radiator were known also as the "3RT" or "London" type. Of these, 60 were made in 1946-7 for West Riding, Devon General, Rhondda, Birmingham, Grimsby, Halifax, Douglas, and Aberdeen; 4,674 in 1946-53 for London Transport; and 40 in 1951 for St. Helens.

About 3,300 others were made in 1946-57 with a high front dash, a long thin radiator more similar to the pre-war Regents, and many other small detail differences, these being sold to a wide variety of provincial customers. Known at first as "0961", these were re-designated as from 1 January 1948 to be "9612E" if fitted with epicyclic gearbox (as most of them were), or "9612A" for the relatively few that had a friction clutch and sliding-mesh gearbox. From 1952, "9612S" referred to those with a new synchromesh gearbox. Some, at the request of certain purchasers, still had the old 7.7-litre engine with sliding-mesh gearbox, and these were known as "0681" at first and "6811A" from 1948. All gearboxes had four speeds. When the legal overall length was increased from 26 ft. to 27 ft. in June 1950 this was met by adding a foot to the rear overhang, thus not affecting the wheelbase, and so creating the "9613E", "9613A", "9613S", and "6812A" types. Also by using different axles all eight models were available 8 ft. wide as well as 7 ft. 6 in.

The single-deck version of the Regent Mark III was made in 1946-57 and known as the "Regal Mark III", the only major differences being the longer 17 ft. 6 in. or 19 ft. 3 in. wheelbase and the high instead of dropped frame behind the rear axle. None were made with the London type of radiator and bonnet. The standard 9.6-litre provincial model, known at first as "0962", became "9621E" from the beginning of 1948 if fitted with epicyclic gearbox, or "9621A" with sliding-mesh gearbox; or (from 1952) "9621S" with synchromesh gearbox. The Regal Mark III was also sold extensively in 1947-57 with 7.7 engine and sliding-mesh and synchromesh gearboxes, as "0682" at first and "6821A" and "6821S" later, but it was not available with the 7.7 and epicyclic. About 2,200 home models were made. For export use, with left-hand controls and 8 ft. wide, there were also the "0963" (later "9631E" and "9631A"), both available with wheelbases of 17 ft. 6 in., 20 ft. or 21 ft. 6 in. to give overall lengths of 27 ft. 6 in., 30 ft. or 31 ft. 6 in.

In December 1949 a completely different "Regal

Mark IV" single-decker was announced, with the then new idea of the engine mounted horizontally under the floor amidships instead of vertically at the front. The existing 9.6-litre engine was turned on its side, with a new crankcase. The Mark IV was designed for higher seating capacity, reduction of noise inside the body, better forward visibility for the driver, outrigger body mounting, and easier engine accessibility and removal. The engine was mounted well off-centre, to the right-hand side, and by using a chain-and-roller hoist permanently fixed to the chassis two men could remove it in 13 mins and refit it in 24 mins. The front axle was a long way back from the front of the chassis, with the radiator just in front of it, and the gearbox (also offset well to the right) was fairly close to the rear axle. At first only the fluid flywheel and epicyclic gearbox version was available, as model "9821E", with either 15 ft. 8 in. or 17 ft. 6 in. wheelbase for 27 ft. 6 in. or 32 ft. (export only) overall length, and 7 ft. 6 in. or 8 ft. width, all with right-hand controls. There was also a left-hand version of the 17 ft. 6 in. model known as "9831E". From June 1950 there was a 16 ft. 4 in. wheelbase model, of both widths, for 30 ft. length, known as "9822E".

A new and even larger 11.3-litre direct-injection horizontal engine was announced in March 1950, based on the 9.6 engine and using the same components to a large extent. It was interchangeable with the 9.6 in all the larger Mark IV chassis. The new engine, also the 9.6 from now on, had two-stage pilot injection, to eliminate diesel knock; it was made under licence from a Swedish firm.

A friction clutch and four-speed synchromesh gearbox became available in January 1952 for the Mark IV underfloor chassis, as models "9821S" and "9822S". A new "Monocontrol" transmission was introduced in the autumn of 1954, with semi-automatic electric operation of the epicyclic gearbox, and finger-tip control, and so the 17 ft. 6 in. and 19 ft. 6 in. models, all 8 ft. wide, became "9825E" with right-hand steering and "9834E" with left-hand. The 15 ft. 8 in. wheelbase model had ceased to be made after 1950, as had the 16 ft. 4 in. and all 7 ft. 6 in. wide models after 1957, but the overseas models continued until 1960.

Two new direct-injection six-cylinder horizontal oil engines appeared in the autumn of 1953. One was the "AH 410", of 410 cu. in. capacity (6.75 litres), and the other was the "AH 470" of 470 cu. in. (7.68 litres), with, however, a different bore and stroke from the earlier 7.7. Later, both were also made in vertical form, as "AV 410" and "AV 470". The Regal Mark IV was a pioneer venture in the unknown field of underfloor-engine layout, and everything had been designed on the heavy side for safety. After a few years of experience it was found that most of the units were too strong. So a new lightweight "Reliance" appeared at the end of 1953, reviving the name of a 1928-30 chassis, and using the "AH 410" or the "AH 470" engine. It met the need for a lighter chassis that would operate with increased economy and yet prove sufficiently robust and reliable to perform all forms of bus and coach service, at any rate in Britain though perhaps not overseas. All models were 30 ft. × 8 ft. with a 16 ft. 4 in. wheelbase. With Monocontrol and air brakes they were known as the "MU2RA" type; with synchromesh and air brakes as "MU3RA"; with synchromesh and vacuum brakes as "MU3RV"; and the export model using the larger engine was "MU3RAE". The Reliance proved to be a highly-successful chassis, and was made in large quantities for more than 20 years. From 1961 onwards a larger AH 590 engine was fitted, as the "Reliance 590" chassis or "2U3RA", with 18 ft. 7 in. wheelbase for 36 ft. length, the AH 590 being a revised version of the horizontal 9.6-litre (590 cu. in.) engine.

Simultaneously with the Reliance in 1953 there also appeared a new "Monocoach". This was of patented integral chassisless construction, developed and built in conjunction with Park Royal Vehicles Ltd for the bodywork. The engine and all mechanical units were identical to those used in the Reliance. The Monocoach also was 30 ft. × 8 ft., with a 16 ft. 4 in. wheelbase. With the AH 410 engine, air brakes and Monocontrol transmission it was model "MC2RA"; with the same engine and brakes but synchromesh it was "MC3RA". The AH 470 engine was normally used only in the export models. Unfortunately the chassisless idea did not prove as popular as was hoped. Sheffield Corporation and Scottish Omnibuses and a few others bought some, but the Monocoach came off the market again after only two years or so. This was no reflection on the excellence of the A.E.C. and Park Royal product, for three other similar joint enterprises of a chassis and a body builder at around this period all met the same disappointment.

Returning to double-deckers, a new "Regent Mark V" appeared in October 1954. It was of traditional layout (the same as previous Regents), and still had a vertical front engine and a half-width driving cab; however its external appearance was very different due to panelling around the radiator and bonnet. Both model "D2RA" (using Monocontrol transmission with air brakes) and the "D3RV" (using clutch and synchromesh gearbox with vacuum brakes) had 9.6-litre engines, and were able to carry bodywork up to a maximum gross weight of 12 tons. There was also a special lightweight model, known as "MD3RV" and restricted to bodywork up to a maximum unladen weight of only 7 tons; this had the smaller AV 470 engine. The Gardner 5LW or 6LW engines could also be used in the D2RA chassis. All four types had a 16 ft. 4 in. wheelbase for 27 ft. length, and either 7 ft. 6 in. or 8 ft. width. By 1956 there was also an "MD2RA" with the AV 470 engine, as well as an "LD2RA" and an "LD3RA" which were 30-ft. long versions of the D2RA and D3RV with an 18 ft. 7 in. wheelbase. All these Regent Vs lasted until A.E.C. ceased making double-deckers in 1968.

A chassisless integral double-decker, known as the "Bridgemaster" was introduced jointly by Park Royal and A.E.C. in September 1956. It was of very low overall height (only 13 ft. 5½ in.), and had central gangways in both saloons and normal seating layout. The new 9.6-litre AV 590 engine was mounted vertically at the front, with a synchromesh gearbox, and a half-cab layout with similar frontal appearance to the Regent V. The rear axle was of double-reduction type with offset drive so as to keep the main shaft at a lower level than the hubs and thus permit a very low floor level. Independent front suspension was used, with wishbones and coil springs, and rear suspension was by radius arms and rubber-bushed trunnions with air bellows. The vehicle was a box-like structure formed by the body framing, with a separate front sub-frame to carry the engine and gearbox. Two models were made, both 8 ft. wide and with rear entrance. One seated 68 in a 27 ft. 8 in. length with 16 ft. 6 in. wheelbase; and the other seated 76 in a 30 ft. length with 18 ft. 10 in. wheelbase. Both were made until 1963. Front-entrance types were also made from 1960.

The "Routemaster" of 1959-67, made to the special order of London Transport, is basically the same as the Bridgemaster, with the same chassisless construction, independent suspension, and 9.6-litre engine, but it is made entirely in aluminium alloy instead of partly steel and partly aluminium, and has a fully automatic gearbox with electro-pneumatic control. There are two versions, with 16 ft. 10 in. and 19 ft. 2 in. wheelbase.

The "Renown", of September 1962 onwards, also has the same independent front suspension and air bellows rear suspension, and the offset-drive double-reduction rear axle to give a very low floor height. But it has a separate chassis frame, and the same AV 590 engine and frontal layout as the Regent V, with an 18 ft. 3½ in. wheelbase and 75 seats.

Control of A.E.C. was purchased by Leyland Motors Ltd, in July 1962, and bus making has now ceased.

The early post-war A.E.C. Regent 0661 differed from pre-war models by its front wing curving round to the bottom of the radiator. This one owned by Reading Corporation had a Park Royal body, and is seen in 1956 at the railway station.

*Left* The 1946 A.E.C. Regal 0662 single-decker had a bonnet and wing as shown here in 1959, as did the Regent, to suit the 7.7-litre engine. This one with Duple coachwork was owned by A. Timpson & Sons Ltd, of Catford, London SE6.

*Below left* A.E.C. built nearly 5,000 Regents with the 9.6-litre engine for London Transport to the special 3RT design, but a further 100 were sold to other operators, such as this one for Coventry Corporation with a Weymann body, seen in 1957.

*Below right* The standard A.E.C. Regent Mark III of 1947-57 was basically similar to the 3RT, except for a higher radiator and bonnet, and very different from the pre-war and 1946 Regents. This one, of 9612A sub-type and with a Weymann body, ran in 1963 for the Charlton-on-Otmoor Service of G. P. Holder in Oxfordshire.

The A.E.C. Regal Mark III of 1947-57 similarly had a larger engine than pre-war Regals, and a different bonnet and radiator. This one, with Alexander bodywork, was part of a large fleet of W. Alexander & Sons (Northern) Ltd, of Aberdeen, seen here at Arbroath in 1963.

The underfloor-engined A.E.C. Regal Mark IV first appeared in 1949. This one, of type 9821E, seen in 1951, had an Eastern Coach Works body and ran for Thomas Tilling Ltd, of London WC1.

From 1950 onwards the law allowed single-deckers to be longer, so the standard A.E.C. Regal Mark IV until 1960 had a longer wheelbase. This 9822E bus in a 1956 picture went to Douglas Corporation on the Isle of Man, and had Willowbrook bodywork.

Experience proved the Regal Mark IV to be too heavy, so A.E.C. produced the Reliance, which remained very popular for many years. This Duple-bodied luxury coach of David Macbrayne Ltd, of Glasgow, is parked in 1959 alongside Loch Fyne at Inveraray.

The A.E.C. Reliance of 1953 onwards was equally suitable for short-stage town bus services, such as this Willowbrook-bodied one for Grimsby Corporation, seen in 1960.

*Right* The A.E.C. Park Royal Monocoach of 1953–6 was a joint enterprise with a bodybuilding firm to produce an integral chassisless vehicle where the body structure carried the main load. Seen here in 1962 is one in the Sheffield Corporation fleet.

*Below left* The A.E.C. Regent Mark V of 1954–68, with modernised frontal appearance, was made with both short and long wheelbase, and rear or front entrance. Here is a long wheelbase Park Royal 72-seater of the East Kent Road Car Co. Ltd in 1963 at Folkestone bus station.

*Below right* A joint enterprise by A.E.C. and Park Royal Coachworks was the double-deck integral chassisless Bridgemaster of 1956–63. Here in 1972 we see one owned by Premier Travel Ltd, of Cambridge, standing in that town's bus station.

# ALBION

*(Scotstoun, Glasgow)*

Albion announced in August 1945 that its "CX 13" or "Valkyrie" chassis was now available and some were already in production; the "CX 9" "Valkyrie" would be available in 1946; and the "CX 19" or "Venturer" should appear about the end of 1945. All three were pre-war models, the CX 9 and CX 13 dating from autumn 1937 and the CX 19 from autumn 1938. Both the Valkyries were a single-deck chassis with 17 ft. 7 in. wheelbase for 27 ft. 6 in. overall length. The CX 9 had a four-cylinder 85 bhp petrol engine, or a four-cylinder 78 bhp direct-injection oil engine, with a space of 23 ft. 9¾ in. behind the bulkhead enabling up to 40 passengers to be seated for bus work. The CX 13 had a six-cylinder 120 bhp petrol engine or a six-cylinder 105 bhp oil engine, with a space of 22 ft. 9¼ in. behind the bulkhead for up to 36 seats for coach work. The Venturer was a 56-seat double-decker with 16 ft. 4 in. wheelbase for 26 ft. overall length. It could only have the 105 bhp oil engine.

A six-cylinder 120 bhp version of the smaller oil engine became available early in 1947, and was fitted into the Venturer double-decker as model "CX 37". It was also put in the new Valiant "CX 39" single-decker with 17 ft. 6 in. wheelbase, which replaced the CX 13. The only large-scale purchasers of the Venturer post-war were Glasgow Corporation, who bought 98, and Red & White of Chepstow and its subsidiaries, but there were other small purchasers elsewhere. The Valkyrie and Valiant sold in large quantities to the Red & White group and in smaller ones to independents throughout Britain; they were not made after 1950.

The largest Albion single-deck model was the "Viking", available from about July 1948. Its 9.9-litre 120 bhp oil engine was really too big for most home users, so far more were sold overseas. The "CX 41 NW" and "CX 41 LW" of 1948, for export only, had wheelbases of 18 ft. 3 in. and 20 ft. 6 in. respectively, for overall lengths of 30 and 33 ft. The "HD 61 N" model of July 1950 was 7 ft. 6 in. wide with 19 ft. wheelbase for 30 ft. overall length and was for home use; "HD 61 NW" was similar but was 8 ft. wide; and "HD 61 LW" was designed for long fast runs overseas, and was 8 ft. wide with 21 ft. wheelbase for 33 ft. overall length. All models had a perfectly straight chassis frame, higher-than-usual ground clearance, vertical front engine and exposed radiator with full-width cab. Vikings were not made after 1951, and Albion withdrew from the full-size chassis market.

The most widely-sold post-war Albion model was the "Victor". The pre-war Victor had a dropped chassis frame with raised front and rear wheelarches, but the post-war Victor was very different, and had a perfectly straight chassis frame both in elevation and in plan. The Victor had a "heavy" robustly engineered chassis; most other makes of smaller chassis were of lightweight and cheaper construction. There was more distinction between heavyweight and lightweight chassis than there is now. The Victor was two feet shorter than the legal maximum length, and designed for only 27 coach or 31 bus passengers. The post-war Victor had a wheelbase of 15 ft. 11½ in. and an overall length of about 25 ft. 6 in. The widely-used "FT 39" model came onto the market in early 1947. It had a new 4.88-litre 75 bhp oil engine with a very smooth action that was almost as good as a high-class petrol engine.

The "FT 3AB" Victor appeared in October 1947. Apart from a 4.26-litre 80 bhp petrol engine, the FT 3AB was similar to the FT 39. The FT 39 was used mainly in Britain and the FT 3AB chiefly overseas, but there were exceptions. They both had a front vertical engine and traditional radiator; they nearly always had a full-width cab, very rarely the more usual half-cab. By contrast with pre-war Victors, the FT 39 and FT 3AB had a more angular radiator with Albion's famous rising-sun trademark cast very large in the top tank. The engine in both models was very small for the size of chassis, making it rather slow in acceleration and hill-climbing, but very economical in fuel consumption; and it could keep a steady 45 mph on the level. The FT 3AB was not made after 1951.

A modified version of the FT 39 Victor, known as "FT 39 AN", appeared at the end of 1951. It had 16 ft. wheelbase, the (same) engine mounted 4¼ in. further forward, and a slightly longer rear overhang, which made room for 33 seats. A dropped rear frame extension could also be provided, either for rear-entrance buses or for luggage accommodation on coaches. By autumn 1954 there was also a 37-seat version, known as "FT 39 AL", with 16 ft. 11½ in. wheelbase and overall length permitting 27 ft. 6 in. bodywork. By autumn 1956 these same two chassis had a larger 5.48-litre four-cylinder oil engine; they were then known as "FT 39 KAN" and "FT 39 KAL" respectively.

In September 1959 two entirely new chassis appeared to replace the FT 39 range. Though still using the name "Victor", they were lengthened to full-sized vehicles, and were the "VT 15 AN" and "VT 15 AL". They seated up to 37 and 41 passengers, with an overall length of up to 27 ft. and 30 ft., and wheelbases of 15 ft. 6 in. and 17 ft. 3 in., respectively; they were only 7 ft. 6 in. wide. These two chassis were again revised in April 1962 when, under the name of "VT 17 BN" and "VT 17 BL", they received the Leyland six-cylinder 0.370 oil engine.

Albion Motors Ltd was purchased by Leyland Motors Ltd in 1951, but for many years afterwards it was still allowed to function independently and to develop new ideas. One of these was the "Nimbus", which first appeared in November 1955. This was a lightweight underfloor-engined single-decker, shorter and smaller than all the horizontal types already on the market. It had a straight frame, orthodox leaf springing, and the front axle set well back so as to leave plenty of room for an entrance in front of it. The Nimbus, known as the "MR9" or "MR9N" type, could seat 31 people in an overall length of only 23 ft. 3 in., with a wheelbase of 11 ft. 10 in., and width of 8 ft. The engine was a new four-cylinder 3.83-litre overhead-valve horizontal unit, designed by Albion but incorporating many features of the Leyland 0.350 engine, and mounted amidships.

In September 1958 the MR9 was replaced by a "NS3N" Nimbus. The length, wheelbase and basic frame remained the same, but a larger 4.1-litre engine was used, again designed by Albion and based on the Leyland 0.350. The width was reduced to 7 ft. 6 in. In September 1960 the NS3N was replaced by an "NS 3AN", which was the same except for its gearbox. A dropped instead of straight frame extension behind the rear springs was also now available as an optional extra. This Nimbus remained on the market until 1965.

Meanwhile in May 1956, after extensive trials on the Kelso-Berwick route, Scottish Omnibuses Ltd announced their own chassisless integral version of the Nimbus. It was made by them at Edinburgh, but all the mechanical units came from Albion, including the then-new horizontal 3.83-litre engine, located amidships with a four-speed synchromesh gearbox; the radiator again tilted at about 45°. Almost the entire body, including the underframe, was of light alloy, giving an unladen weight of 3 tons 9¼ cwt. Extra rigidity to the body was provided by the steel seat frames, which formed a direct link between the sides of the vehicle and the main underframe members. The bus was 24 ft. long, with 32 seats, and an unusual 7 ft. 9 in. width. Dunlop rubber suspension, with the axles located by radius arms, was used instead of orthodox leaf springs.

A heavier underfloor-engined chassis was also developed by Albion. The prototype in 1955 had an orthodox visible radiator at the front, but when the production model of the "Aberdonian" or "MR 11L" appeared in October 1957 it had the radiator under the floor tilted at about 45°, the same as the Nimbus. The Aberdonian had a 16 ft. 4 in. wheelbase for 30 ft. overall length and was 8 ft. wide. The general layout and appearance of its chassis was the same as an elongated Nimbus. The standard Leyland 0.350 horizontal engine was used. Although the Aberdonian was selling quite well it was withdrawn from the market in 1961, and nothing replaced it, apart from the Leyland Tiger Cub.

After having been out of the double-deck market for about ten years, and despite having been owned by Leyland for ten years, Albion very surprisingly re-entered it in November 1961 when it announced a "Lowlander" double-deck chassis. This followed the current fashion of having an extremely low frame and floor, as close to the ground as possible. It had a separate chassis and was not an integral vehicle. The engine and radiator were in the orthodox front position, with a half-width cab; it had the same fibreglass frontal structure as was then used on the Leyland Titan PD2, blending from the cab-front and grille into the bonnet top and nearside wing. The Leyland 0.600 (i.e. the PD2) engine was used, and the transmission was also standard Leyland units. There were two alternative Lowlanders, either the

"LR1" with fluid coupling and pneumo-cyclic gearbox, or the "LR3" with friction clutch and four-speed synchromesh gearbox.

The rest of the Lowlander however was very different from the Titan. The main frame, as well as being very low and reasonably orthodox on the offside, had its nearside main member bulged outwards for several feet in front of the rear axle – nearly to the full width of the vehicle. This was in order to accommodate the gearbox, keep it well clear of the central gangway, and get the gangway floor down to slightly lower than the top of the gearbox (the floor under several seats here was slightly higher). The Lowlander had an overall height of only 13 ft. 5 7/8 in. unladen. The wheelbase was 18 ft. 6 in. with overall dimensions of 30 ft. × 8 ft.; it could seat up to 74. The entrance was at the front, and to keep the floor here extremely low it was not possible to use an orthodox chassis frame member 8¾ in. deep as was done on the offside. Instead, there were two members, side by side, of channel sections 7 in. and 5½ in. deep. There was thus an unbroken level floor from the entrance step to the extreme rear of the bus, and a single-step 15¼ in. high entrance, almost level direct off the pavement.

In August 1962 two additional Lowlanders were introduced. These were the "LR5" (with fluid coupling and pneumo-cyclic gearbox) and the "LR7" (friction clutch and synchromesh). Both had semi-elliptic springs at the front, but air suspension at the rear; this brought the overall height down even lower, to only 13 ft. 3 7/8 in. Lowlanders were made only until 1965, but in those four years they sold quite well.

*Above* The Albion Venturer CX19 of 1945-7 was the double-deck version of the CX13, using the same engine and bonnet. Here in 1962 we have one with a Weymann body owned by the Cheltenham District Traction Co., seen outside the firm's garage.

*Right* The Albion Valkyrie CX39 of 1948-51 had a new and larger engine, with access holes in the bonnet side. The Blue Bus Service Ltd, of Windsor, Berkshire, owned this one with Reading bodywork seen in 1960 at Maidenhead.

The Albion Victor FT39 was sold extensively in 1947-59 as a smaller chassis than the Valkyrie. This one of Green Luxury Coaches Ltd, Walton-on-Thames, Surrey, is parked in 1950 at Hastings near the Fish Market, and has Allweather bodywork.

One of our smallest underfloor-engined buses was the Albion Nimbus of 1956-63. This one, the NS3N sub-type, with Willowbrook body, is passing through the village of Shere in 1963 on the Forest Green to Guildford bus route of A. T. Brady (Brown Motor Services) of Forest Green, Surrey.

## *Albion*

The prototype of the full-sized underfloor-engined Albion had the radiator at the front. It appeared in 1955 and was operated by the Western S.M.T. Co. Ltd, of Kilmarnock, Ayrshire, in this 1955 picture. Bodywork was by Scottish Aviation.

The production model of the underfloor-engined Albion Aberdonian of 1957-60 had the radiator under the floor further back. David Lawson Ltd, of Kirkintilloch, Dunbartonshire, used this one on their "Round Scotland" tour. It is parked at Strome Ferry in 1959, and has an Alexander body.

## *Albion*

Albion re-entered the double-deck market in 1961-5 with the Lowlander, with a very low floor height. Southend-on-Sea Corporation, Essex, bought ten of them, with bodywork by W. Alexander, as pictured in 1963.

After Albion became a Leyland subsidiary in 1951 several large batches of the parent's Titan chassis were sold to Glasgow Corporation under the name of Leyland Albion. Here in 1962 we see an Albion PD3 with Alexander bodywork in Cathedral Square.

# ATKINSON

*(Preston, Lancashire)*

Atkinson did not make buses until September 1950, when the "Alpha" appeared, as an underfloor-engined single-decker. Atkinson built their own chassis frames, braking linkages, and driving cabs for lorries, but fitted a wide variety of other units made by specialist companies, including twelve different types of engine. This policy was also adopted for the Alpha bus, which was similar in general layout to most other underfloor-engined buses of the Fifties. The frame was perfectly straight in side view, with no wheelarches, but in plan view it was narrower at the front end. It had the Gardner 6HLW horizontal engine, with David Brown gearbox and Kirkstall hypoid rear axle.

The home model, or "PM 746H", of which the first two went to the North Western Road Car Co. Ltd, had a 16 ft. 6 in. wheelbase for 30 ft. × 8 ft. bodywork; the overseas "LPL 746H" model had 17 ft. 6 in. for 31 ft. 6 in. By September 1952 an alternative "PM 745H" was also available, with the Gardner 5HLW. A lightweight version of the Alpha appeared in the summer of 1953, with a main frame of 7 7/8 in. section × 2¾ in., instead of 8 in. × 3 in. All other dimensions and units were the same, with two alternative engines, the 5HLW or the 4HLW, which made "PL 745H" and "PL 744H" respectively. All four models were still on the market until 1965.

Atkinson introduced their first, and only, double-decker, the "PD 746", in August 1954. It was of orthodox layout, the same as most buses of the Thirties, and was designed to satisfy a demand for a lightweight chassis for either central- or rear-entrance bodywork. The engine was the Gardner 6LW, and the wheelbase was 16 ft. 6 in. for a 27 ft. length. One was sold to Stalybridge.

Atkinson made a few bus chassis in 1950-55. This underfloor-engined Atkinson Alpha with Willowbrook bodywork, owned by R. I. Davies & Son Ltd, of Tredegar, Monmouthshire, is seen in 1966 in the town centre.

# AUSTIN

*(Longbridge, Birmingham)*

In March 1947 a 26-seat normal-control "CXB" coach chassis of which a few had been made in 1939 was again marketed, with a 15 ft. wheelbase, 25 ft. overall length, and a 3½-litre petrol engine. A forward-control version of this, with the same wheelbase and same engine, known only as the Austin "Coach" chassis, appeared towards the end of 1948. As the demand for coach chassis was then so great that neither Austin nor other makers could cope, many small operators fitted coach bodywork (for up to 26 seats) on the standard Austin 5-ton truck chassis, unmodified.

Production of the forward-control "Coach" did speed up, however, and eventually it became a common sight in most parts of Britain, and plenty were sold overseas too. A larger 4-litre petrol engine was fitted by the end of 1949, and the Perkins P6(V) could be fitted from 1953 onwards. Bodywork was usually by Mann Egerton, for a 26-seat coach, or by Mulliner for a 30-seat bus. This was as many as could be held under British regulations, but by using eight rows of 3-&-2 seating instead of seven of 2-&-2 it was often possible to get up to 42 seats in the same body shell in some foreign countries.

Austin withdrew from the home market after 1954, as it was concentrating on trucks. But towards the end of 1956 a new Austin "Series III Coach" chassis appeared, for export only. It had a different frontal appearance and radiator grille though still the same wheelbase and of forward-control with 26 ft. 2½ in. length; it remained on sale for many years. Alternative engines were the 4-litre Austin petrol, now uprated to give 87 bhp instead of 68, or a new 5.1-litre B.M.C. diesel engine.

The Austin CXB normal-control bus and coach chassis of 1947-54 was based on the 5 ton goods chassis. Here in 1967 we see one of Beestons (Hadleigh) Ltd, with Plaxton bodywork, standing outside the operator's garage at Hadleigh, Suffolk.

The forward-control version of the Austin passenger chassis was made in 1949-54, with several different frontal appearances. This one in 1951 was owned by Garner's Coaches (Fox & Hart Ltd), of South Ealing, Middlesex.

# B.M.M.O.

*(Bearwood, Staffordshire)*

The Birmingham & Midland Motor Omnibus Co. Ltd, usually known as B.M.M.O. or as Midland Red, is a large operating company which started in 1905. From 1922 to 1940 they manufactured all their own bus and coach chassis at Bearwood, near Smethwick, and also made some of the requirements of six other operating companies in the B.E.T. group. Since 1945 although they have bought some chassis from Guy, A.E.C., and Leyland, they have again made most of their own chassis, but none for any other operators. In 1936-9 they pioneered three experimental prototype rear-engined single-deckers (later converted to underfloor layout), and also one chassisless underfloor bus in January 1946.

This vehicle, the "S5" type, was built in conjunction with Metropolitan-Cammell-Weymann, whose all-steel bodywork relied on the steel panelling to stiffen the chassisless chassis. Even the roof panels were part of the structure, and the engine, gearbox, springs, axles, steering etc, were supported directly by the floor frame. All the mechanical units were of conventional design, and the engine was B.M.M.O.'s own pre-war 8-litre six-cylinder diesel, mounted on its side towards the offside just behind the front axle. The radiator was in the orthodox front position, with the passenger entrance between the radiator and front wheels. There were 40 seats, all facing forwards.

B.M.M.O. was highly satisfied with this design, and with only minor alterations they made 100 of "S6" type in 1947-8. After increasing the width from 7 ft. 6 in. to 8 ft., they made 100 of "S8" and 100 of "S9" type in 1948-9, and 155 of "S10" type in 1949-50. Bodies for some of these were made by Brush as well as M.C.W. From 1 June 1950, 30 ft. single-deckers were allowed to run in Britain, and the very first such vehicle licenced, on that same day, was a lengthened version of the B.M.M.O. underfloor-engined bus, type "S11"; 44 of this 44-seat design, modified to "S12", entered service from September onwards. Twelve luxury coaches and 45 express coaches (types "C2" and "C1") were also made in 1948-50.

Meanwhile B.M.M.O. had produced a new $10\frac{1}{2}$-litre oil engine, which in October 1950 they put in a new light-alloy integral underfloor single-decker of quite different design, involving a new constructional technique, and with independent front suspension and rubber-bush rear suspension. The monocoque body construction gave an immensely strong underframe, with 44 seats, the entrance in front of the wheels, and no separate cab. The unladen weight was 5 ton 18 cwt, which was one ton less than the S12 of the same 30 ft. × 8 ft. size. This new "S13" entered mass production, but after a few years B.M.M.O. ceased making their own chassis and now buy standard types from the commercial market.

*Left* For many years the Birmingham & Midland Motor Omnibus Co. Ltd made its own chassis and engines, or its own mechanical units for fitting into chassisless bodywork made to B.M.M.O. designs by Brush and M.C.C.W., such as this S10 type of 1949-50 working a local town service at Shrewsbury in 1956.

*Far right* The B.M.M.O. horizontal underfloor engine and mechanical units were also used in the long-distance coaches built by Duple for the Birmingham to London express service of the Midland Red.

# BEADLE

*(Dartford, Kent)*

By 1939 this bodybuilding firm were interested in chassisless or integral bus construction, and took out several patents, with a view to going into production. At that time extremely few buses or coaches had been built in which the body and chassis were made as one unit instead of two separate items, and London Transport (trolleybuses) and Midland Red were the only people who had tried. Beadle's plans were delayed by the war, but in 1945-6 they built four prototype 33-seat single-deck buses in which advantage was taken of the lighter weights obtainable by eliminating the chassis and using aircraft methods of body construction with light alloy materials. The result was so successful that they then shed yet further weight in the mechanical components, by the use of smaller and lighter engines, gearboxes, axles, etc, which led to attractive economies in lower fuel consumption and increased tyre life. The price, although more than for ordinary mass-produced small buses, compared well with standard 35-seaters on heavy chassis.

New engines and gearboxes were not available at this time, so secondhand overhauled units were used, in conjunction with certain operators. Four different makes were chosen, to prove that the Beadle system could be used with any of them. The first prototype had Commer

mechanical parts and a Commer petrol engine, ex Eastern National, and re-entered service with Eastern National at Chelmsford in October 1945. The second used Leyland Cub parts and a Gardner 4LK oil engine, and entered service with Southern National at Taunton in August 1946. The third had Bedford OWB parts and a Bedford petrol engine and went to Eastern National in December 1946; and the fourth used Dennis Ace parts and Gardner 4LK engine. All four were extremely economical to run.

The first prototype had all-steel bodywork, and the other three had light alloy bodywork which was 27 cwt lighter so that the weight of the fully-laden bus was over 3 tons less than the legal maximum of 9 tons. All four were built to a 1946 patent specification for a method of underframe and floor construction which lent itself to receive any suitable type of engine and transmission units, and also permitted the use of standardised bodies without adaptation. The main structure was formed of four longitudinal and eight transverse members welded together to form a cellular framework, with diagonal cross bracings. It was later found that the rest of the structure was so stiff that the diagonal bracing was not needed.

In 1947-9 about 60 Beadle buses were built, mostly with Bedford units, and operated by the Eastern, Western, and Southern National companies, Eastern Counties and others. Also 24 buses with old Leyland Cub units were made for Lincolnshire, and in 1949 a batch with brand-new Morris-Commercial units and Saurer engine was made for Bristol and elsewhere. In 1950-1 a larger type was evolved, using engines and units from scrapped pre-war A.E.C. Regal and Regent buses and Leyland Tigers and Titans. These ran both as 39-seat buses and 35-seat coaches, 30 ft. × 8 ft.; large quantities were made. Maidstone & District took 76, East Kent 31, Southdown 20, East Yorkshire 10, and various others. Simultaneously, Beadle was also working in conjunction with Sentinel, as described elsewhere.

All the above vehicles had a vertical front engine and visible radiator. In 1949 a Beadle integral bus with an underfloor engine mounted amidships was produced. Soon afterwards the Beadle company was purchased by the Rootes group, and in 1952 the Beadle Integral Bus or

Coach was placed onto the general market for sale outside of the Tilling and B.E.T. groups. Two standard models were now advertised. One had the Commer $4\frac{3}{4}$-litre petrol engine with 17 ft. 6 in. wheelbase (Commer was also owned by Rootes), and the other had the Perkins P6(V) $4\frac{3}{4}$-litre oil engine with 17 ft. 11 in. wheelbase. Both types were 30 ft. long. The Commer-engined model had small tyres (8.25-20) and could carry only 39 passengers; the Perkins-engined model had larger tyres (9.00-20) and could carry 41.

In 1954, when the new Rootes TS3 two-stroke diesel engine appeared, these two Beadle models were withdrawn and replaced by a new 16 ft. 6 in. wheelbase integral vehicle in which the TS3 engine was mounted horizontally under the floor. This had 41 seats as a coach, or 45 as a bus, within the 30 ft. × 8 ft. limit. But the floor loading height was rather high above the ground, being 3 ft. $4\frac{3}{4}$ in. on this Beadle as compared with 3 ft. on the previous Perkins-engined Beadle and 2 ft. $6\frac{1}{2}$ in. on the equivalent Commer chassis with the same Rootes engine. The 41-seat coach had a front hinged or centre sliding door and weighed 5 tons 14 cwt; the 45-seat bus just had an open front entrance and weighed only 5 tons 5 cwt, which was very much less than most other single-deck buses. The body was made entirely of light alloy. Production ceased about 1957 and Beadle went out of business.

*Above* Beadle incorporated all the mechanical units of 24 pre-war Leyland Cubs into some new chassisless vehicles they made in 1947-8 for the Lincolnshire Road Car Co. Ltd. Here is one of them in Louth town centre in 1955.

*Far left* Beadle also made a larger type of chassisless coach in 1950-55, using engines, gearboxes, axles, etc. from scrapped pre-war Regals, Regents, Tigers, and Titans. This one, with 1937 Leyland Tiger TS7 units, ran for the Scout Motor Co., of Hastings, Sussex, as seen in 1959.

*Below* Beadle chassisless production in 1954-7 mostly incorporated brand-new mechanical units, made by Commer, with the Commer TS3 two-stroke oil engine. This one seen in 1958 was owned by Birch Brothers Ltd, of Kentish Town, London NW5.

# BEDFORD

*(Luton, Bedfordshire)*

Bedford was one of only three firms (the others were Guy and Daimler) which were allowed to make bus chassis through most of World War II. It was announced in August 1942 that a large number of the intended 1939 Bedford 32-seaters were now being built for the Ministry of Supply. Nobody had made any single-deck buses for well over two years, as Guys and Daimlers were all double-deck, and there was an urgent need for new single-deckers throughout the whole of Britain. The new chassis, known as the "OWB", was a large lightweight chassis, being an elongated version of the normal-control 1935 WTB 26-seater. It was by far the largest lightweight bus chassis that had yet been made.

The OWB was an immediate success, and many thousands were made over the next four years. All had utility bodywork to a standard Ministry design, mostly built by Duple, but Mulliner, Scottish Motor Traction, and Charles H. Roe also built some. It is probable that more buses to this one design were made than to any other one design at any period of time. The wheelbase was 14 ft. 6 in., overall length was 24 ft. 4 1/8 in., width 7 ft. 6 in., rear overhang 7 ft. 3 in., overall height laden 8 ft. 10¼ in., and interior height 6 ft. 1½ in. It had a folding door at the near-side front, emergency door at the rear, eight pairs of forward-facing wood-slatted seats on each side (one was in front of the door and alongside the driver), and only one opening window on each side. The engine was basically a 13-year-old design, a six-cylinder overhead-valve model of 1929 of which many thousands were used in all Bedford buses and lorries all through the Thirties. With only minor improvements this has continued in regular production right up to today, being one of the most successful engines ever made.

From October 1945 onwards the OWB was re-designated "OB", but continued in large-scale production. The 32-seat service bus continued, now known as "Mark II", but with upholstered seats, domed roof panels, a sliding door, and five half-drop windows per side; it was still made by Duple and Mulliner. For luxury coach work the 29-seat "Vista" body appeared in January 1946; many operators used it for bus work as well. From then until 1951, many thousands were made by Duple, also by S.M.T., though some OBs did have other types of bodywork by other makers.

The new "SB" or "Big Bedford" chassis appeared in September 1950, the biggest vehicle Bedford had yet made. It was a forward-control model with full-width cab, but (unusually until that time) no separate bulkhead. The wheelbase was 17 ft. 2 in., for a length and width of 27 ft. 6 in. and 7 ft. 6 in. A new 4.93-litre petrol engine was used (300 cu. in.), developing 110 bhp. The main frame was fairly low, upswept over the axles. The engine and radiator were still at the front, but instead of being externally visible as on all previous Bedfords and most other makes until that time the radiator was now hidden behind bodywork panelling, a feature which was adopted by many other makers around then.

Mass-produced bodywork, either as the "Vega" 33-seat luxury coach or as the "Mark VI" 33-seat service bus, but differing only internally, was provided by Duple and used by most operators, though several other firms, notably Burlingham and Plaxton, did also make some bodies for the SB. From September 1951 SBs 8 ft. wide were introduced. By lengthening the body to 28 ft. 11¾ in., with a longer rear overhang, both the Vega and the Mark VI were able to have 37 seats from September 1952, and a new "Super Vega" with extra luxury features also appeared, all three now being of either width. A 40-seat all-metal Duple service bus also appeared two years later, and at this time an alternative engine became available in the form of the Perkins R6(V) diesel.

In September 1956 the wheelbase was increased to 18 ft., and the tail of the chassis was chopped off behind the rear axle, so that the bodybuilder had to provide extra support here. This made the complete vehicle 30 ft. long and with 41 seats. The main frame now had a flat top throughout, making it 2 ft. 6¾ in. off the ground when laden instead of 2 ft. 4 in. From 1957 onwards four alternative engines were available: the Bedford 300 cu. in. petrol; a brand-new Bedford 300 cu. in. diesel having the same bore and stroke as the Bedford petrol; the Perkins R6(V) diesel; and the Leyland 350 cu. in. 0.350 oil engine. The chassis with these engines were thereafter known as types "SB3", "SB1", "SB0", and "SB8" respectively. The Perkins engine ceased to be fitted from 1958, and in December 1961 the new Bedford 330 cu. in. diesel engine became available as chassis type "SB5", in place of the 300 diesel. The SB8 was dropped in 1965, but SB3 and SB5 (Bedford's own petrol and oil engines), with the 18 ft. flat-topped frame and the Vega and Super Vega 41-seat bodies are still being made today.

The 29-seat OB had been replaced in 1951 by the 33-seat SB which was gradually enlarged to 37 and 41 seats. After a few years Bedford realised there was still a need for a smaller passenger chassis, and so when a new 6-ton goods chassis was put on to the market in February 1957 a modified forward-control version of this for passenger work appeared eight months later. This was the "C4Z1" if fitted with the Bedford 3.52-litre petrol engine (the same engine as the OB and OWB had had, but now uprated from 84 to 100 bhp), or the "C4Z2" if using the Bedford 300 cu. in. diesel (the same as the SB1). In both cases the wheelbase was 13 ft. 8½ in. for 23 ft. 6 in. overall length and 30 seats. The new chassis was usually fitted with Duple coachwork, in conjunction with Bedford, and this combination rather confusingly re-used the same name of "Vista". Several other firms also supplied bodies independently.

Many detail improvements were made to this chassis at the end of 1961, and it was re-designated "VAS1" with the 300 cu. in. diesel engine and "VAS2" with the 3.52-litre petrol. It was now virtually a short-wheelbase version (still 13 ft. 8 in.) of the SB. At the end of 1967 the VAS1 was replaced by a "VAS5" using the new 330 cu. in. Bedford diesel engine; this and the VAS2 are still in production today.

A completely new chassis, known as "VAL", appeared in September 1962. It had unorthodox twin-steering six-wheel layout, with four wheels at the front (with single tyres) and two wheels at the rear (with twin tyres). Though Bedford had never tried it, this layout had been common for some time on heavy lorries of many other makes, but nobody had ever used it on any passenger vehicles except for Leyland with its Gnu of 1938-9, of which only eight were made. All previous six-wheeled buses and coaches (and there had been very few after 1932) had had four wheels at the rear and two at the front. The VAL thus had eight tyres, which helped to distribute the load better, and also enabled the wheels to be smaller than on a conventional chassis, only 16 in. dia. with 8.25-16 tyres. This enabled the main frame to be lower, only 29¾ in. laden despite being straight throughout with no wheelarches. Moreover the twin-steering layout, where all four wheels on a pair of axles followed correct geometric steering, gave far less wear and tear on the tyres than with the older rigid six-wheeler where the four rear wheels were dragged sideways when rounding a sharp corner.

The VAL was 36 ft. long, taking advantage of the newly increased legal maximum length permitted from the end of 1961. This enabled VAL to have up to 55 seats in a single-decker, which was more than most double-deckers had had (usually 50 to 52) about 32 years previously. In those same 32 years the Bedford had risen from being the smallest single-decker then on the market, to being the largest single-decker. The wheelbase of the VAL from the "front front" axle to the rear was 19 ft. 3 in. with 3 ft. 11 in. between the two front axles; the width was 8 ft. It had a Leyland 0.400 diesel engine as none of the standard Bedford engines were large enough. The VAL, and also the VAS, had an unusual transmission brake as well as the ordinary wheel brakes. Like all other Bedford chassis the VAL proved extremely popular and sold in large quantities, and was in production until 1973.

After the war the Bedford OB with Mark II Duple bodywork of 1945-51 was basically the OWB but improved in many small details, notably curved panelling and softer seats. Odiham Motor Services Ltd owned this one, seen in 1954 in the main street of Odiham, Hampshire.

*Far left* This Bedford OWB was owned by Mid-Wales Motorways Ltd, of Newtown, Montgomeryshire, and was seen in 1960.

*Above* The Bedford OB chassis was also supplied in vast quantities in 1946-51 with standardised Duple Vista coach bodywork, of which J. L. Green, of Thorney, Cambridgeshire, owned this example in 1960.

*Below* The Bedford SB, the biggest chassis as yet made by Bedford, usually had this standard Duple Vega bodywork in 1950-54. W. H. Patch, of Stamford, Lincolnshire, used this one on his Cream Bus Service from Stamford to Peterborough, where we see it in 1960 at the terminus.

## *Bedford*

The Bedford SB with longer wheelbase and overall length, also improved frontal appearance and Duple Super Vega (or other) bodywork was made from 1952 onwards. This one, parked in 1961 at Kirkcudbright, was owned by W. & A. Campbell, Gatehouse of Fleet, south-west Scotland.

For bus work, rather than coaching, the Bedford SB was also supplied from 1954 onwards with this semi-utility standard Duple bodywork, again involving a different frontal appearance. This one was with the Greyhound Service of T. D. Alexander, Arbroath, County Angus, in 1963.

The Bedford C4Z1 and C4Z2 of 1957–61 were a short 29-seater introduced after the SB had been lengthened to 41 seats, but the frontal appearance (in several variations) was the same. David Macbrayne Ltd used them on the Isle of Skye, as seen in 1959.

The Bedford VAS was an improved version of the C4Z made from 1961 onwards, and the J4LZ, shown here in 1963 with the Sutherland Transport and Trading Co. Ltd, at Lairg, was almost identical.

The Bedford J2, although only a forward-control conversion of the 3-ton tipper chassis, was used extensively for 19- or 21-seat coaches. This one with Plaxton bodywork ran for W. L. Bird & Son, of Theddingworth, near Market Harborough, Leicestershire, and was seen in 1966.

The twin-steering Bedford VAL six-wheeler of 1962 onwards was one of the largest single-deckers ever used in Britain until then. The Embankment Motor Co. (Plymouth) Ltd used this one in Devonshire. It has Plaxton bodywork, and is seen here in 1973 in Plymouth's bus station.

# BRISTOL

*(Brislington, Bristol)*

After the war Bristol resumed production somewhat earlier than most manufacturers, in fact five months before the war had finished, as the Ministry of Supply allowed Bristol to augment the Guy and Daimler output. The Bristol "K6A" double-deck chassis of February 1945 was similar to the last pre-war model, but used the A.E.C. 7.7-litre oil engine instead of the Gardner 5LW, and the radiator was smaller and lower. The wheelbase was 16 ft. 3 in., for a 26 ft. overall length, with a chassis of straightforward orthodox layout suitable for 56-seat bodywork (26 down plus 30 up) made by several different firms.

After the first 300 had been made a supply of Gardner 5LW engines began to arrive, so K-type chassis fitted with this engine were known as "K5G", the same as about 840 pre-war chassis. A few also used the Gardner 6LW engine, and these were known as the Bristol "K6G" chassis. This longer engine involved moving the bulkhead back, and reduced the body space from 21 ft. 6 in. to 21 ft. Under the Ministry of Supply's allocation scheme many chassis found their way into the fleets of operators who had never previously had any Bristols. By the spring of 1946 a single-deck version of the same chassis, but with 17 ft. 6 in. wheelbase for 27 ft. 6 in. overall length and 36 seats, was also in production, and these were known as type "L6A", "L5G", or "L6G" according to which engine was fitted. The simple design and robust construction of K and L chassis enabled them to run for well over 100,000 miles between major overhauls.

In August 1948 the new Bristol "AVW" direct-injection 8.15-litre engine became available, designed and made by Bristol Tramways at Brislington, near Bristol. Although a completely new design, its basic layout was very typical of most other bus oil engines, and because of its simplicity it soon entered large-scale production. Apart from mounting brackets, and the use of 24-volt electrical equipment instead of 12, the Bristol engine was interchangeable with the A.E.C. and Gardner in both K and L chassis, and drove through the same gearbox and differential with the same ratios. Chassis fitted with it were known as types "K6B" and "L6B". Gradually, as production of the Bristol engine speeded up, so fewer chassis were fitted with A.E.C. engines and more with Bristols, but the two Gardner types continued in substantial quantities, and certain customers working in flat territory, such as Eastern Counties, took a few single-deckers with four-cylinder Gardner engines, thus creating the "L4G" chassis.

From 1 July 1946 8 ft. wide buses were legally permitted but at first not all customers wanted them. When Bristol made the wider chassis they were known as types "KW5G" and "KW6B" for the double-deckers, and "LW5G" and "LW6B" for the single-deckers. None of the 8 ft. chassis had A.E.C. engines. From 1 June 1950 the legal maximum length of double-deckers was increased from 26 ft. to 27 ft., and of single-deckers from 27 ft. 6 in. to 30 ft. Bristol now made buses of both lengths and both widths, intermixed. The longer double-deckers were types "KS5G" and "KS6B", and the longer single-deckers were "LL5G" and "LL6B". Those that were both wider and longer were types "KSW5G", "KSW6B", "LWL5G", and "LWL6B". To accommodate the extra length Bristol's wheelbase was increased to 17 ft. 6 in. for Ks and 19 ft. for Ls, now seating 64 and 40. The six-cylinder Gardner engine was used only rarely in the shorter chassis, but much more so in the long and wide ones, which thus became "KSW6G" and "LWL6G".

In their hey-day the various forms of "K" and "L" were amongst the most numerous of all British bus types. A total of about 3,010 double-deckers and 2,180 single-deckers were sold for home use, almost entirely in England and Wales. None ever went to Scotland, except just four Ks and ten Ls to the Caledonian of Dumfries, and 15 Ls to Edinburgh. Apart from the first few hundred just after the war, when the Ministry was allocating them to customers under wartime regulations, when some (mostly Ks) were sold to various municipalities, their sale thereafter was restricted only to the big companies in the B.E.T. and Tilling groups. In practice the only substantial deliveries to B.E.T. companies were to Maidstone & District and North-Western, before the sales were further restricted to just the ex-Tilling companies as a result of the voluntary nationalisation of the Tilling group and its sale to the British Transport Commission in 1949. Bodywork in 1945-7 was by various firms, but from 1948 onwards it was almost exclusively built by Eastern Coach Works Ltd of Lowestoft, Suffolk, to very standardised designs, E.C.W. being also bought by B.T.C.

Bristol has never done much export business, either before or after the war, and has never had any export-only models. But they did in 1949 sell 100 standard L5G buses to Hyderabad, India; also 46 Ls in 1948 and 100 LWL6Gs in 1950 to various operators in South Africa.

Undoubtedly Bristol's greatest contribution to bus chassis development, and the first real departure by any manufacturer in 20 years from the traditional layout of the double-deck chassis, apart from the A.E.C. "Q" in 1934, was made in October 1949 when Bristol introduced its new "Lodekka" or "LDX" chassis, in conjunction with E.C.W. The design was destined to have far-reaching effects on the industry as a whole. Until now all covered-top double-deckers with a central gangway upstairs had been about 14 ft. 6 in. high. You could not get any lower without sacrificing headroom for people standing inside, and so falling foul of the Ministry of Transport's Construction and Use Regulations. Most bus operators had some routes which went under railway bridges lower than this. You could reduce the bus height to about 13 ft. 6 in. by offsetting the upper-deck gangway so that the feet of the people standing in it were lower than the heads of those standing downstairs in the centre, but this involved the nuisance of long seats upstairs with four people on each, and people on the near-side being trapped by three others and unable to get out. And you could not put the lower-deck floor any lower, because the space beneath it was needed for the propeller shaft to transmit the engine power to the back axle.

The Bristol-E.C.W. Lodekka solved the problem. It still kept the engine and radiator at the front, with the gearbox immediately behind it, but by offsetting the drive inside the gearbox it was possible to move the output shaft well over to the off-side, very close to the main chassis frame. This left enough space on the centre-line for the gangway to be dropped down into a well, below the floor level under the seats, and 12 in. lower than the floor of a normal bus. The whole of the upper-deck floor could thus be brought down, keeping the gangway in the centre instead of at the side, so you could still have 2-&-2 seating. The prototype Lodekka was 13 ft. 4 in. high unladen, or 13 ft. 2 in. laden. Not only could it now get under lower bridges, its centre of gravity was also reduced, so it was less top-heavy; the floor was only 16½ in. above the road. The floor frame was integrated with the chassis frame structure, eliminating the usual separate body crossmembers, and the body framework, which was wholly of light alloy, was supported directly by the full-width crossmembers of the chassis. The wheelbase was 15 ft. 11 in., and length and width were 26 ft. × 7 ft. 6 in. Maximum road speed was only 34 mph, and the engine was the standard Bristol AVW.

One prototype was operated by Bristol itself, the other by West Yorkshire. In February 1951 the transmission was redesigned to bring the differential unit further forward, to just behind the gearbox instead of half-way along the chassis. From here two separate drive shafts, one on each side of the chassis as before, led to a separate final drive each end of the rear axle. The length and width were increased to 27 ft. and 8 ft.

In this revised and highly unusual form the Lodekka went into mass production with a first batch of 200, of which 45 were coded "LD5G", 62 "LD6G", and 93 "LD6B". As with the K and L types, these codes show which engine was fitted. The design proved highly successful, and many thousands more were built, with each of the three engines, and operated extensively by all the B.T.C. (ex-Tilling) bus companies, also the Scottish and Red & White groups. From 1960 the 27 ft. model (with 16 ft. 11¼ in. wheelbase) was known as type "FS", and a 30 ft. model with 19 ft. 2¼ in. wheelbase was introduced as type "FL". The Gardner 6LX engine was now available as well as the 6LW, and minor alterations to Bristol's AVW engine had produced the "BVW". By 1965 the AVW and BVW had vanished, but the Leyland 0.600 engine could be fitted as well as 6LX. There were now also front-entrance versions of the 27 footer and 30 footer, known as "FSF" and "FLF", i.e. "FSF6G", "FSF6L", "FLF6G" or "FLF6L" to indicate the engine. Bodywork for all types has always been made by E.C.W.

Turning to single-deckers, in February 1951 the prototype appeared of the Bristol-E.C.W. underfloor-engined integral 30 ft. × 8 ft. model. The first one was made of light alloy and weighed only 5 tons 12 cwt, but it was later agreed that light alloy would not be used on the production model, due to its scarcity, and that these would weigh almost 6 tons, or 8 tons 12 cwt with 42 passengers. The prototype had the standard AVW engine, but it was turned on its side and had external modifications. The radiator was just in front of the engine. It was planned to go into production as a 40-seat bus with front and rear doorways, or a 42-seat bus with a front doorway only, all bodywork to be made by E.C.W. and for use solely by B.T.C. companies.

However, after testing the prototype, it went into production in April 1952 as a 39-seat luxury coach weighing 7 tons empty. The first one went to Crosville, and averaged 17 mpg at a steady 35 mph, using the 6HLW Gardner engine. The wheelbase had been lengthened, to 17 ft. 2 in., and the radiator moved forward to just behind the front axle. Bus bodywork of 45 seats followed later, weighing 6 tons 6 cwt. The frame was deliberately made very high off the ground, 3 ft. 6 in. when laden, so as to provide a flat floor with no large wheel boxes, and all seats facing forwards. The Gardner 4HLW or 5HLW were used for bus work, and the horizontal AVW became available later. The chassis was known as the "LS" type, or "LS4G", "LS5G", "LS6G" or "LS6B" depending on which engine was fitted. The all-welded underframe and running units were assembled at Brislington, but this did not constitute a strong-enough self-contained chassis, so temporary side stiffening pieces had to be added before driving the 240 miles to Lowestoft to complete the body, and this incidentally provided a good road test for each chassis. Many thousands of LS buses and coaches, and of the subsequent but similar "MW" underfloor-engined type, were made before being replaced by other types in 1966.

From about 1954 to about 1964 Bristol also made a smaller lightweight bus known as the "SC" type for secondary routes. It had a vertical Gardner 4LK engine. The wheelbase was 17 ft. $4\frac{1}{2}$ in., with 28 ft. × 7 ft. 6 in. length and width.

*Above right* The Bristol LL5G of 1950-56 was the long-wheelbase version of the L5G. This one, with E.C.W. bus bodywork, owned by Crosville Motor Services Ltd is parked in 1960 at Llanidloes, Montgomeryshire.

*Far left* The Bristol K6A of 1945-7 had an A.E.C. engine. This one, owned by Colchester Corporation, Essex, and seen here in 1964 at St John's Green with Duple bodywork, was one of the relatively few to be outside the Tilling group.

*Right* This Bristol LL6B, with Bristol engine and long wheelbase, has the standard E.C.W. coach body, with full-width cab and concealed radiator, which could equally well be used on the LL5G. This one is with Hants & Dorset Motor Services Ltd at Bournemouth bus station in 1956.

*Left* Most Bristol K5Gs of 1946-50 had a standard Eastern Coach Works body (as here) and most ran for companies in the Tilling group, as did this bus which was in the Westcliff-on-Sea Motor Services Ltd fleet and was seen in 1958 at Hullbridge, Essex.

## *Bristol*

The Bristol Lodekka LD6B of 1951 onwards was an outstanding technical achievement, vastly different from any previous chassis. This one also is with Hants & Dorset at Bournemouth bus station in 1960. Bodywork was always by E.C.W. Earlier models had the deep radiator shown here, but later this was shortened.

The Bristol Lodekka FLF of 1962 onwards had the shorter radiator, a longer wheelbase and overall length, and front entrance instead of rear, but the same basic structure. One owned by the Eastern National Omnibus Co. Ltd, of Chelmsford, is seen in 1962 at Victoria coach station, London.

## *Bristol*

The Bristol E.C.W. underfloor-engined LS-type integral single-deck bus of 1952 onwards is seen here in 1958 under Eastern National ownership at Euston Square, London.

Various refinements to the LS type produced the MW type, seen here in 1959 as an MW6G with the standard E.C.W. luxury coach body, owned by Wilts & Dorset Motor Services Ltd of Salisbury, and parked at Hartley Wintney.

The Bristol SC was a smaller type of single-decker of integral but straightforward layout, with standardised forward-control E.C.W. bodywork. The Eastern Counties Omnibus Co. Ltd had a large fleet of them at Peterborough, as seen here in 1960.

# COMMER

*(Luton, Bedfordshire)*

In June 1946 the new Commer "Commando" went into production, as a 26-ft. long single-decker with 15 ft. 9 in. wheelbase. It had the bonneted normal-control layout, with a body length behind the engine of 21 ft. 9½ in. This was enough for a 28-seat coach or 32-seat bus body, which were made by several firms, and large quantities operated all over Britain. In addition 375 had an unusual 1½-deck body layout that was never used on any other normal-control chassis; these were made by Park Royal and used by the R.A.F. and several air lines. The Commando had the pre-war Commer 4.08-litre petrol engine, or the Perkins P6(V) diesel.

In the autumn of 1948 the "Avenger" appeared. This was of forward-control layout, with a new 4¾-litre petrol engine in the usual longitudinal position at the front, but by mounting it low down and tilting the cylinders over at an angle of 66° to the vertical it was possible to keep it sufficiently low to be under the cab floor, giving a full-width cab without the normal interruption of a bonnet in the middle, and so two passengers could be seated alongside the driver. Although not a true underfloor-engined chassis in the way that 13 other makes subsequently were, the Avenger was always described and advertised as if it was. But it was two years earlier than any of these mounted amidships. A special feature was the chromium deposit over the full length of each cylinder bore to retain the oil in microscopic fissures, the surface being four times as hard as cast iron, which gave life of over 200,000 miles with negligible cylinder wear. Like the Commando, it also had a straight un-arched chassis frame, with a low extension at the rear, and a 15 ft. 9 in. wheelbase. Overall vehicle length was 27 ft. 6 in., with 22 ft. body space behind the driver.

The Avenger was a best-seller for many years, and standard bodywork was made by Plaxton, Harrington, Churchill, and (later) Yeates, in conjunction with Commer and sold jointly. Various other firms also supplied suitable bodywork, mostly seating 32 to 35. The radiator was hidden behind an ornamental grille, but this grille was supplied by Commer, and not by the bodybuilder as in the case of all other makes of single-decker. It almost always had four long and 16 short horizontal chromium mouldings, and hence an Avenger was much easier to identify than most other underfloor-engined vehicles.

In April 1954 Commer at Luton, in conjunction with Tilling-Stevens at Maidstone, started mass-producing the revolutionary new Rootes "TS3" engine. This three-cylinder horizontally-opposed two-stroke oil engine with blower scavenging was for use in the Avenger chassis, also in Beadle and Harrington chassisless passenger vehicles and in the larger Commer vans and lorries. It was the most unconventional British-designed compression-ignition engine ever offered for road transport use. It had two opposed pistons in each cylinder bore, no inlet or exhaust valves, and a combustion space formed between the crowns of each pair of pistons.

The TS3 engine was shorter than the petrol one so it used less body floor space in the Avenger chassis. At the same time an alternative longer and wider Avenger was put onto the market, with 17 ft. 6 in. wheelbase and 30 ft. overall length by 8 ft. width, to seat up to 41. The TS3 engine proved highly successful despite its many unusual features, and was made in large quantities. The petrol-engined and short-wheelbase versions of the Avenger were not made after 1956, but the TS3-engined long-wheelbase model continued until about 1964. Commer then, surprisingly, withdrew from the bus and coach market, after having been one of the most important suppliers for over half a century.

As well as the Beadle (see elsewhere in this book) an integral chassisless bus or coach body, made in aluminium alloy throughout, and incorporating the Commer engine, gearbox, transmission, and axles, etc, was also made and sold by Thomas Harrington Ltd of Hove, Sussex. In effect the Harrington light-alloy "Contender" vehicle was really a chassisless Avenger, with a 15 ft. 7 in. wheelbase and 30 ft. × 8 ft. length and width for 41 coach or 45 bus seats. It was in production from September 1952 to about 1957. The entrance could be either front or central, and unladen weight was only 4 tons 12 cwt. It was advertised in 1951-3 with the 4¾-litre petrol engine, and in 1954-7 with the TS3 two-stroke oiler.

In addition, in 1956-7 (only) Harrington also advertised

an integral chassisless coach using a Rolls-Royce six-cylinder petrol engine (with 15 ft. 5 in. wheelbase for 27 ft. 6 in. overall length), and one using a Rolls-Royce straight-eight-cylinder B80 petrol engine (with 16 ft. 2 in. wheelbase for 30 ft. length), with either A.E.C. synchromesh or Rolls-Royce epicyclic gearbox. Both engines were mounted underfloor amidships. Some of these vehicles may have been sold for overseas use, but it is doubtful if any ran in Britain.

The Commer Commando of 1946-9 was a normal-control chassis of traditional layout. This one was owned by Streamways Tours Ltd of Penarth, Glamorganshire, in 1950.

The Commer Avenger of 1948-64 had the engine tilted over at an angle and mounted underneath the floor of the driving cab. Most of them, no matter who built the body, had the arrangement of polished mouldings on the front grille as seen here. This one with Allweather bodywork was owned by C. H. Bird, of North Hykeham, Lincolnshire, in 1960.

### *Commer*

This Commer Avenger, with Plaxton's standard bodywork as used also on Ford and Bedford chassis, was one of the few not to have the usual horizontal mouldings. It was owned in 1958 by Lucky Line Coaches, Wilkinson & Crief, Edgware, Middlesex.

The chassisless integral Contender of 1952-7, made by Thomas Harrington, the bodybuilders of Hove, Sussex, used Commer Avenger units for all mechanical parts. This one, owned by Audawn Coaches, of Corringham, Essex, was seen in 1972.

# CROSSLEY

*(Stockport, Cheshire)*

Crossley was one of the first firms to get started on bus work again after World War II, and in June 1945 their new 8.6-litre oil engine was announced. The prototype had been tested for nearly two years in a Manchester bus, and, due to an improved design of combustion chamber, it gave much better fuel economy than the pre-war Crossley engine.

After various minor changes the standard post-war Crossley double-deck chassis became known as type "DD42/7" for the 7 ft. 6 in. width and "DD42/8" for the 8 ft. width, both having a 16 ft. 7½ in. wheelbase for the 26 ft. overall length. The standard single-deck bus chassis were similarly "SD42/7B" and "SD42/8", and the coach chassis was "SD42/7C", all with 17 ft. 7 in. wheelbase for 27 ft. 6 in. length. The double-decker and the coach had a dropped rear frame, and the single-decker was straight. All chassis were of conventional straightforward layout, with vertical engine and half-width cab, with many small differences from the pre-war Crossley, and a new and much narrower radiator giving a quite different frontal appearance. Crossley themselves built the bodywork used on most of their chassis, and they also built on other makes as well.

In December 1945 Crossley received Britain's biggest-ever export order for buses; 1,175 single-deckers for the Netherlands State Railways, comprising 250 articulated "PT42/1" 80-seaters, 500 rigid "SD42/1" 48-seaters, and 425 rigid "SD42/2" 38-seaters. The tractor portion of the 250 was the standard double-deck chassis, but with shortened wheelbase (to 11 ft.) and converted to normal control. All three types used the 8.6-litre engine, but the 48-seaters had it supercharged to increase its output by 50% and give a 60 mph road speed. The 48-seaters had a 20 ft. 3½ in. wheelbase, 35 ft. 6½ in. × 8 ft. overall dimensions, and a substantial front projection beyond the front axle, the engine and radiator being in the usual front vertical position. The 38-seater, with 18 ft. 0½ in. wheelbase and 32 ft. 4¾ in. length, later became a standard Crossley export model.

Meanwhile from 1945 onwards Crossley double-deckers sold extensively to most British municipal fleets, though not to many companies. The single-deckers also went mostly to municipalities, though Western Welsh took a large quantity. The coaches sold extensively and almost exclusively to smaller independents. From January 1950 onwards a new system of air induction gave the 8.6-litre engine more power and economy. In 1950 some 30-ft. long coaches were made, as model "SD42/9".

A Crossley speciality was the use of the hydro-kinetic turbo-transmitter made by Brockhouse Engineering (Southport), Ltd. Crossley offered this device as a third alternative to the constant-mesh and the synchromesh gearbox in all their double- and single-deck chassis. A prototype had been running with Manchester Corporation for two years. South Shields ordered six double-deckers thus fitted in July 1943, of which the first one was delivered (and demonstrated to the press) in February 1946. The bus was controlled solely by one accelerator pedal, also a foot brake, but no clutch pedal. There was a complete absence of jerk or vibration on starting, even on a hill of 1-in-11. But by not having a gearbox to use the engine as a brake when descending hills the brake-shoe wear was up to 50% more, also the fuel consumption was 10% more. However maintenance was cheaper and the bus was much easier to drive. Luton Corporation also ordered eight, as later did several other municipalities, but some of them subsequently removed the turbo-transmitters and fitted ordinary gearboxes instead; indeed some even removed the Crossley engines and fitted other makes of engine.

Despite the apparent success and prosperity of the Crossley business, it sold out to A.E.C. unexpectedly in 1948, after only three years of hectic post-war activity. Existing models continued to be sold less actively for another three or four years until they were withdrawn altogether. The name was then kept alive for much longer than the vehicles, as by September 1950 the standard A.E.C. "Regent Mark III" range of double-deckers was already being marketed under the name of "Crossley Mark III", identical save only for the badge on the radiator. Likewise the standard A.E.C. "Regal Mark IV" underfloor-engined single-deckers (a layout which Crossley itself had never had) were marketed and advertised as "Crossley Mark IV". By 1952 they became "Crossley Regent Mark III" and "Crossley Regal Mark IV", and the entire A.E.C. range was also offered as "Crossleys" until at least 1958. A.E.C. even published a sales pamphlet about the "Crossley Bridgemaster" when this new model first appeared in the autumn of 1956. But no buses were actually sold under this false name, and it was rather unkindly suggested that A.E.C. did it so as to give them an extra Stand at the various Commercial Motor Shows. Bodywork was still made at Stockport, also some B.U.T. (as successor to A.E.C.) trolleybus chassis, until the end of 1958, when the factory was closed and sold.

The Crossley DD42/7 chassis of 1945-51, with Crossley's own bodywork as well, is seen here in 1949 in the ownership of Portsmouth Corporation, Hampshire, outside Fratton Church.

The Crossley SD42/7 single-deck of 1945-51, also with Crossley's own bodywork, had the same bonnet and nearside wing arrangement as the double-decker. This one, owned by J. W. Wood, of Mirfield, Yorkshire, is about to enter Dewsbury bus station in 1959.

For the last year or so of production both double- and single-deck Crossleys had this improved style of radiator with more polished metal. This one, with Duple bodywork, was owned by H. Webster, of Pattishall, Northamptonshire, and is parked in 1963 in Leighton Buzzard.

# DAIMLER

*(Coventry, Warwickshire)*

Soon after the outbreak of war in 1939 all manufacturers had to cease making buses and turn over to tanks or army lorries. However by 1942 most bus operators were so urgently in need of new vehicles that the Ministry of Supply allowed just three firms to start making buses again, and Daimler was one of these. The famous COG5 design (Commercial, Oil-engined, Gardner, five-cylinder), of which many thousands had been made in 1933-40, came back into production from December 1942 onwards; it was now known as the "CWG5" type (W for wartime). Still much the same as pre-war, it had a few small austerity sacrifices, such as heavy cast iron instead of lightweight elektron for the crankcase, and the omission of the decompressor from the engine.

The Gardner 5LW oil engine was still used, and this drove through the surprising luxury (for wartime conditions) of the fluid flywheel and Wilson gearbox which had been standard on all Daimler buses since 1930. Double-deck bodywork was made to austerity Ministry of Supply specification by several different firms, and the vehicles were allocated to operators by the Ministry of War Transport. The wheelbase was 16 ft. 3 1/8 in., and the overall length 26 ft.

Only the first 100 wartime Daimlers were of CWG5 type; thereafter the A.E.C. 7.7-litre oil engine was fitted, the chassis being type "CWA6"; about 1,260 were made in the next two years. On the CWA6 a sheet-steel radiator shell with wire-mesh grille was used instead of the nicely-polished aluminium casting of the COG5 and CWG5, although the famous fluting was still retained. In May 1945 Daimler started to make its own new oil engine, the CD6 type, and chassis fitted with it became the "CWD6" type. Development of the CD6 had started in 1936, but in the 1940 Coventry air-raid the prototype and all drawings and records were destroyed, so in 1943 Daimler started again. It was an 8.6-litre direct-injection unit designed to last two years or 100,000 miles between overhauls. Unusually, all auxiliaries were driven from the rear end of the crankshaft instead of the front. The CD6 weighed 19 cwt in 1945, but it was hoped to get this down to 17 cwt when aluminium would be available instead of cast iron. Fuel consumption was 16 mpg on a non-stop 25 mph run, or 8 mpg with five stops per mile. Subsequent experience made this one of the most successful of British bus engines.

Production of the Daimler engine was at first very limited, and most chassis were still fitted with the A.E.C.; but gradually more and more CWD6s and fewer and fewer CWA6s came off the Coventry production line, though the CWA6 did not entirely cease. The engine, transmission, and general layout of the wartime CWA6 made this bus very similar to the pre-war A.E.C. Regent. The only major difference between the three types of Daimler chassis apart from the engine and radiator was in the rear axle. When viewed from the front the starting-handle hole was exactly in the centre of the radiator on the CWD6, slightly to the off-side on the CWG5, and slightly to the near-side on the CWA6.

In April 1946 Daimler opened a new factory extension at Allesley, two miles west of the main Coventry plant. It was hoped bus production would soon be four times the pre-war level. Daimler had already received orders from 32 British operators for the CWD6, several of them for over 100 chassis; 40% of the output would go to export. As soon as wartime restrictions were relaxed, and more aluminium was available, the CWD6 chassis was given many small improvements, now becoming the "CVD6" type (V for victory). A.E.C. engines were dropped in 1947, except for special orders, as plenty of Daimler engines were now being made, but Gardner 5LW engines again became available, in a chassis known as "CVG5".

By the spring of 1947 Daimler was making single-deck buses as well as double, and the CVD6 and CVG5 were each available in four different forms. With 17 ft. 2½ in. wheelbase for 27 ft. 6 in. single-deckers and 35 seats; 19 ft. wheelbase for 30 ft. single-deckers and 41 seats; 16 ft. 3 1/8 in. wheelbase for 26 ft. double-deckers and 56 seats; and 17 ft. 6 in. wheelbase for 27 ft. 6 in. double-deckers and 64 seats. The 6LW Gardner was also available in double-deckers from 1947, and in single-deckers from 1950, as "CVG6". The longer-wheelbase models were sold only for export (mostly South Africa) until 1950, when the law allowed them to run in Britain.

The 6LW (only) was also used in a 70-seat 18 ft. 8¾ in. wheelbase 30-ft. long export double-decker from 1948.

All the above types (except the 70-seater) were 7 ft. 6 in. wide at first, and also available 8 ft. wide from 1948. On all models from February 1952 onwards an alternative to the exposed radiator was available in the form of curved panelling sweeping round from the cab front to the bonnet side, with the Daimler fluting in a chromium-plated "eyebrows" effect, the first buses to have this being 40 for Coventry Corporation. With minor exceptions all the above single-deck variations remained in production until about 1953 and the double-deckers until about 1965. From September 1952 there was also a special lightweight chassis, with more aluminium, various simplifications, and its tail cut off. It was available only as a double-decker with 16 ft. 4 in. wheelbase and 7 ft. 6 in. wide. This could have the CD6 or the 5LW engine, as "CLD6" and "CLG5" types, weighing only 4¼ tons instead of 4¾ tons. The first two were sold to Birmingham and the Potteries. From July 1956 the 30 ft. double-decker for home use was improved in many details, with 74 seats, and wheelbase slightly reduced to 18 ft. 6 in. It was now known as the "CVG6-30" type, and supplied with the curved front panelling only. The 27 ft. 6 in. double-decker was now known as "CVG6-27" type. These two chassis were still made until about 1970.

In October 1948 Daimler produced the largest and most powerful bus engine ever made in Britain either before or (with two exceptions) subsequently. This was the "CD650" type, of 10.62 litres and developing 150 bhp, being an enlarged version of the CD6. It was fitted into a new "CD650" double-deck bus chassis with 16 ft. 4 in. wheelbase for 56 seats and 27 ft. × 8 ft. wide. It had hydraulic power-assisted steering (the first on any British bus) with the mechanism incorporated inside the steering column. This chassis was of conventional half-cab layout, with an enormous prominent radiator. It sold extensively in many parts of South Africa, but was too powerful for British use, although the Blue Bus Service in Derbyshire ran several for many years.

A 20 ft. wheelbase single-deck CD650 chassis was also made, and sold extensively in Brazil and elsewhere, but none ran in Britain; and a 17 ft. 6 in. wheelbase double-deck CD650 was made from the end of 1949. Also in 1949 Daimler produced a six-wheel double-deck version of the CD650, of which 20 were sold to Cape Town, and these were the only six-wheel double-deckers of any make made in Britain after 1938. A 22 ft. wheelbase "CVD650-220" single-deck chassis for 36 ft. bodywork and 64 seats was introduced in September 1958, using a supercharged CD650 engine giving 200 bhp, and this chassis was also available, as "CVG6-220", with the new Gardner 6LX.

The new "Freeline" underfloor-engined single-decker was announced in May 1951. It had been under development for two years, but was held back so as to incorporate the new larger legal dimensions. It was now to go into production with alternative 16 ft. 4 in. and 17 ft. 6 in. wheelbases for 30 ft. and 32 ft. overall lengths, and both 7 ft. 6 in. and 8 ft. widths with both left- and right-hand steering. The engine was a horizontal version of either the Daimler CD650H or the Gardner 6HLW. From October 1954 a new 20 ft. 4 in. wheelbase 35 ft. long Freeline for overseas was available. The CD650 engine in both horizontal and vertical form ceased to be made in 1965, but all Daimler chassis formerly using it continued to be available with the new Gardner 10.45-litre 6LX or 6HLX engines, in addition to the smaller and older 6LW or 6HLW. The Daimler CD6 engine ceased in 1965 in favour of 6LW or 5LW.

The new rear-engined double-deck "Fleetline" or "CRG6-30" appeared in October 1960, and has been a best-seller ever since; it is now one of only three British double-deckers still being made. With a short 16 ft. 3 in. wheelbase and 30 ft. overall length, it could seat up to 78; overall height was only 13 ft. 4 in. There was a very low flat floor downstairs, a central gangway in both saloons, and a wide entrance forward of the front axle only 12½ in. above the road. The engine was the Gardner 6LX, mounted vertically and transversely across the rear.

From 1965 the 6LW engine was available as an alternative in the CRG6-30 chassis, and a new "SRG6-33" chassis was introduced with an 18 ft. 6 in. wheelbase for 33 ft. overall length and up to 86 seats, or up to 45 if fitted with a single-deck body. For Walsall Corporation a special "CRG6-27" was made, only 27 ft. long, with the front end shortened in front of the standard wheelbase.

*Above left* The first 100 Daimlers built in 1943 were the CWG5 type with Gardner engine. This one, with Duple utility bodywork, went to Swindon Corporation, Wiltshire, where it is seen in 1956.

*Above right* This Daimler CWA6 of 1943-6, owned by Aberdeen Corporation, Scotland, also had a Duple body, and is seen in 1955 in Commercial Street.

*Left* In single-deck form, and with a Willowbrook body, this Daimler CVD6 of 1947-53 ran for the Venture Transport Co. (Newcastle) Ltd, of Consett, County Durham, as seen in 1959.

*Right* The Daimler CVD6 double-decker of 1946-65 with Daimler engine and Charles Roe bodywork was bought by Cleethorpes Corporation in Lincolnshire. Here we see a 1950 model at Isaacs Hill in 1960.

*Below right* An alternative frontal styling, with the bonnet blending into the wing and the cab front, was available on all Daimlers from 1952. This 1962 CVG6 with Roe bodywork was bought by South Shields Corporation.

*Below left* The Daimler CD650 of 1948-53 had a big 150 hp engine and extra-large radiator. It was far too powerful for most British operators, and most of them were exported. One of the very few that stayed in Britain ran for Rossie Motors (Rossington) Ltd, near Doncaster, Yorkshire, as seen in 1955, with Burlingham bodywork.

## *Daimler*

The rear-engined Daimler Fleetline double-decker of 1960 onwards has been a best-seller. This Roe-bodied example for Sunderland Corporation was photographed in 1962 when brand new in the Jaguar works at Coventry.

With the engine at the rear of the Daimler Fleetline it is worth looking at the rear end of this one owned by the Stalybridge Hyde Mossley and Dukinfield Transport and Electricity Board in Hyde market place, Cheshire, in 1972. The radiator grille can be seen at the offside rear. Bodywork was by N.C.M.E.

# DENNIS

*(Guildford, Surrey)*

The famous Lancet single-deck bus of 1931-9 reappeared in June 1945 as the "Lancet III" or "J3", substantially unchanged except for using the new Dennis "06" 7.58-litre oil engine instead of the pre-war "Big Four" petrol engine. The chassis was of conventional layout for 36-seat 27 ft. 6 in. bodywork, with a 15 ft. 5 in. wheelbase, and half-cab frontal layout; it gave 11¼ mpg on rural bus work. Some had the Gardner 5LW engine, making them "J4" type. An 18 ft. 6 in. wheelbase version for 40 seats and 30 ft. length ("J10" type) came in autumn 1950. In March 1949 a 21 ft. 6 in. wheelbase export version for 46 seats and 35 ft. length appeared; this was the "Lancet IV", and it had a full-width cab still with the 06 engine. A shortened version of the full-width cab Lancet IV for home use appeared a year or two later. The export model was made until 1962, and the three home models until 1955.

The pre-war double-deck Lance reappeared in 1946 as the "Lance III" or "K3". It had many minor improvements, also a larger radiator and the 06 engine, but it was basically similar to the Lancet. The wheelbase was 16 ft. 3¼ in. for 56-seat 26 ft. bodywork. The biggest user of Dennis buses was always the local Aldershot & District Traction Co. Ltd, which for many years bought Dennis exclusively. Although A. & D. used the 06 engine in the K3 chassis, most other Lance users preferred the Gardner 5LW, for which a "K4" chassis was made. Aldershot also later took some of these K4s which had panelling that curved from the cab front to the bonnet side similar to Guy and Daimler changes at the same period. The Lance was made until 1954, though never in vast quantities.

The underfloor-engined single-deck "Dominant" chassis, 30 ft. × 8 ft., appeared in September 1950. Most major firms at around this time were introducing new underfloor-engined chassis, an entirely new field, and all of them played for safety and made them too heavy and robust. Dennis did also, and only two Dominants were made before a new "Lancet UF" appeared just two years later. This had a wheelbase of 16 ft. 4 in. instead of 16 ft. 9 in., the main frame being 9 in. × 3 in. instead of 10 in. × 3 in.; it weighed 78 cwt instead of 97 cwt. The frame of the Dominant was straight throughout, except for small humps over both axles and over the engine. The Lancet UF frame was 3 in. higher, so as to eliminate these humps and keep the main central part straight, but the front and rear ends beyond the axles were dropped down very close to the road. Therefore the driver and all his controls were now at a much lower level than the passengers, and a rear-entrance (or front) bus with low loading platform was possible. The horizontal 06 engine was still used, but an ordinary Dennis gearbox was fitted instead of the Hobbs semi-automatic transmission. The Lancet UF remained on the market until 1962.

Turning to the smaller lightweight chassis, the pre-war "Falcon" came back in 1948, with the same 16 ft. 6 in. wheelbase for a 26 ft. 6 in. length, and a new 17 ft. 7 in. wheelbase model (for 27 ft. 6 in.) was added. Both could be either normal-control bonneted, or forward-control with half-width or full-width cab. Four alternative engines could be fitted: the Dennis 3.77-litre petrol, the Gardner 4LW or 4LK oil, or the Perkins P6(V) oil. Both wheelbases were replaced in September 1950 by a 17 ft. 1 in. (for 27 ft. 6 in.) Falcon, with a new Dennis 5-litre oil engine, forward control with full-width cab, and no separate bulkhead. Bodywork for this, and for most other smaller Dennis chassis, could be made by Dennis itself if required. Two years later the 5-litre engine was replaced by another new Dennis oiler, a 5½-litre model giving 87 bhp instead of 75. Falcons were made until about 1956, being replaced by the Pelican.

The new lightweight underfloor-engined "Pelican" appeared in September 1954, using a horizontal version of the same 5½-litre engine. The wheelbase was 16 ft. 4 in., for 30 ft. × 8 ft. bodywork and up to 44 seats. The main frame members were perfectly straight in both plan and elevation for their whole length, including the long extensions beyond both axles. But they were rather closer together than usual, and this enabled the driver, as on the Lancet UF, to sit at a lower level than the passengers, so as to give them a clear forward view over his head. To do this he was sunk in a well outside the off-side frame member, and with his feet below it. The wheelbase was shortened by 2 in. two years later. The Pelican vanished after 1958, since when Dennis has made hardly any single-deckers for the home market, and has concentrated mainly on fire engines and refuse-collecting vehicles, with a few ordinary lorries.

In the double-deck bus field, however, Dennis had a revival. In 1951, Bristol had introduced their new Lodekka which had proved highly successful, but for political reasons was for sale only to the nationalised Tilling and Scottish groups of companies. Because of its very low floor height many municipalities, also several of the B.E.T. companies and larger independents, wanted to buy the Lodekka but were not allowed to. So Dennis negotiated a licence by which they were authorised to make the Lodekka at Guildford, but under the name of "Loline", for sale to anybody who wanted them. Only the longer 30 ft. × 8 ft. version with 18 ft. 6 in. wheelbase was made at first, as there was now less demand for the original shorter one. By incorporating some existing Dennis components into the basic Bristol design, the first chassis was completed in September 1956 – only six months after the original announcement. Dennis used the Gardner 6LW engine, and by adapting their own standard five-speed gearbox they did not need the separate transfer gearing which Bristol had fitted on the Lodekka.

Available initially only for rear-entrance bodywork, a front-entrance Loline was made from the end of 1958 onwards. This had a 19 ft. wheelbase, with 6 in. shorter rear overhang. To provide extra stability and strength at the front entrance, the two main side members of the unit-construction chassis of this "Loline Mark II" were spaced much wider apart than on the Mark I, with far steeper up-sweep to pass over the front axle. Also from the end of 1958 the Gardner 6LX engine or a new Dennis 8-litre unit could be fitted instead of the 6LW, and the shorter 16 ft. 8½ in. wheelbase models for 27 ft. overall length were now available for both rear and front entrances as well as the longer type. From September 1960 the wheelbases of these two later models were increased to 19 ft. 2¼ in. and 16 ft. 11¼ in., under the name of "Loline Mark III", with many small improvements, notably air suspension for the rear wheels. Lolines were sold extensively to many municipalities, and to the Aldershot, North-Western, and other companies, but production ceased in 1967.

The Dennis Lancet J3 of 1945-55 was of orthodox half-cab layout but used the new Dennis oil engine. This one, with bodywork by Windover of Hendon, was owned by the Yorkshire Traction Co. Ltd, of Barnsley, and is seen in 1950 at Stamford on the 200 mile London to Keighley service.

The Dennis Lance of 1946-54 was available with a Gardner engine, as type K4. Here is one in Aldershot bus station in 1956, with East Lancs bodywork.

Only two underfloor-engined Dennis Dominants were made as prototypes in 1950. One went to Aldershot & District, with Strachan bodywork, and is seen in 1958 at Streatham.

## *Dennis*

The Dennis Lancet U/F underfloor-engined single-decker of 1952-62 was evolved from the Dominant, and a fair number were made. Newport Corporation, Monmouthshire, took a batch, with bodywork by D. J. Davies of Merthyr Tydfil. Note the unusual rear entrance, and the very low driving position, in this 1960 picture.

The Dennis Falcon of 1948-56 appeared in three different forms. Here it is a normal-control 20-seater with bodywork by Dennis itself, owned by the East Kent Road Car Co. Ltd, and parked at Hythe in 1959.

Ten forward-control half-cab Dennis Falcons with 30-seat Dennis bodies were used by Southdown Motor Services Ltd at Havant, Hants, mainly for crossing the weak bridge onto Hayling Island, though this one, seen in 1956 outside Havant Railway Station, hopes to be making a longer trip.

## *Dennis*

This Dennis Falcon with full-width cab and long wheelbase, almost a full-size bus, ran for the Yellow Bus Service of Sidney Hayter, of Stoughton, near Guildford, Surrey, as seen in 1955. Some Lancets also had this frontal appearance.

The Dennis Loline of 1956 onwards was a slightly modified version of the Bristol Lodekka, made under licence. Here in 1963 we see the long-wheelbase rear-entrance version with East Lancs bodywork as used by Aldershot & District, outside their Hindhead garage.

The Dennis Loline Mark II of 1958 onwards had a front entrance, a totally different form of structure for the underframe, and a different radiator and frontal appearance. This one in 1963 was owned by Reading Corporation, Berkshire, and had an East Lancashire body.

The 1947 type of A.E.C. Regent 0661/20 in the fleet of the Trent Motor Traction Co. Ltd, with Willowbrook bodywork, stands in Alfreton bus station, Derbyshire, in 1962.

An A.E.C. Regent Mark III 0961 type of 1948, with Park Royal bodywork, owned by Morecambe & Heysham Corporation, Lancashire, standing at the Heysham Road, Morecambe, terminus in 1962.

# DODGE

*(Kew, Surrey)*

Before the war, Dodge chassis were assembled in Britain from components made by the parent company in the U.S.A. The new range of Dodge vehicles after World War II was entirely Kew designed and British made, but Dodge did not make their own oil engines.

Dodge activities since the war have been mainly in goods vehicles, with buses and coaches only a small sideline. The "86/P6" bus chassis appeared in October 1950, but was for export only. It had a 15 ft. 10 in. wheelbase, for 27 ft. overall length, with semi-forward-control layout, and used the Perkins P6(V) engine. This was uprated from 79 to 83 bhp in 1954, and the chassis became "87/P6". From January 1962 this was replaced by a new 16 ft. 2 in. wheelbase chassis for 41 seats, which could have either the Dodge petrol engine as model "3087" or the Perkins "Six-354" as "3087P"; there was also an 18 ft. 45-seat chassis with either the Perkins R6(V) engine as model "3090R" or the Leyland Comet "0.350" engine as "3090Y".

Dodge buses did not become available for British operators until September 1962 when a 15 ft. 10 in. wheelbase model with 42-seat Metro-Cammell body was launched. This had the unusual combination of a vertical engine in the front, alongside the driver, with the front axle set back and the entrance in front of this alongside the engine. This gave the driver good control over fare collection, but the layout was very cramped and congested, with not enough floor area between the engine and the entrance steps. Maudslay had tried the same layout in 1937, with similar lack of space. The new Dodge used the Leyland "0.370" 6-litre engine or the Perkins "Six-354" 5.8-litre unit. The main frame was straight for its entire length in both plan and elevation. This "KS 700" bus remained on sale in Britain for eight years, but not many were sold, though the overseas models continued to sell well.

In the acute post-war shortage of new buses Southend-on-Sea Corporation purchased five Canadian Dodges in 1945 and ran them for ten years, possibly the only overseas-built psvs to enter service anywhere in Britain at any time between about 1930 and 1970. This one is outside the Corporation garage in 1953.

The Dodge coach chassis as made in Britain from 1962 onwards is seen here in 1964 at the Kursaal, Southend-on-Sea, in the ownership of Charles Rickards Ltd, Brentford, Middlesex, and has Strachan bodywork.

# FODEN

*(Sandbach, Cheshire)*

Following extensive research with the pre-war prototypes, Foden announced two new bus chassis in August 1945. They were entirely new – not just modified goods chassis. In their main features these double- and single-deck models were almost identical, but they differed in wheelbase (16 ft. 3 in. and 17 ft. 6 in.), and in overall length (26 ft. and 27 ft. 6 in.). Both had orthodox forward control, with vertical front engine and radiator and a half-width cab. A striking external appearance was given by hiding the radiator behind a grille and by some panelling which curved round to incorporate the front of the cab, the top of the bonnet, and the whole of the near-side wing, all in one smooth sweep. All other double-deck makers did something similar to this in later years, but Foden was the first.

The Gardner 5LW oil engine was standard but at a loss of 6¼ in. of body space the 6LW was available. A large single-plate clutch of 15¾ in. diameter was fitted, with a unit-mounted gearbox of, normally, four speeds all in constant mesh, but a special super-low gear of 9.9 to 1 was available as an extra for very hilly districts. The main frame was extremely strong, with prominent diagonal cruciform cross-bracing. The steering column was unusual, being inside a massive aluminium tube which supported it rigidly from the chassis. Double deckers with 5LW and 6LW engines were designated "PVDD5" and "PVDD6", and single-deckers with the 5LW and 6LW were "PVSC5" and "PVSC6". Longer versions of this chassis became available in 1948, for export only, with 19 ft. 6 in. and 21 ft. wheelbase for 30 ft. and 33 ft. bodywork.

In September 1948 Foden made headlines by introducing its own new oil engine, which became available in all Foden bus and lorry chassis as an alternative to the Gardner. Moreover the Foden was on the Two-Stroke principle, almost the only manufacturer ever to do this. The piston compressed the air on every upward stroke, and was driven down by the explosion on every downward stroke, instead of the usual suction, compression, expansion, exhaust sequence of a four-stroke engine. The Foden Diesel, or "FD6" engine, was based on the Kadenacy principle, and was a supercharged two-cycle c.i. engine of 4.09 litres swept volume, with a low-pressure Roots-type blower.

Despite its high power (126 bhp) the engine was so small and compact that Foden claimed that in getting the utmost power out of the smallest box they had outdistanced all their rivals on both sides of the Atlantic. The diesel knock was much quieter than usual, but the whine of the supercharger was rather loud. The double- and single-deck chassis with the new engine were known as types "PVDE6" and "PVFE6". They could cruise at 55 mph despite the legal maximum of 30, and had a fuel consumption of 15 mpg, hence the two-stroke method did not involve higher fuel consumption.

In September 1950, Foden introduced a rear-engined chassis at a time when everybody else was trying underfloor engines. The Foden was the first rear-engined bus or coach chassis offered by any British manufacturer for normal production, though Leyland had made 49 to the special order of London Transport in 1939. With the engine at the front valuable passenger space was lost, and noise from the engine was carried through into the body. Foden claimed that if the engine was under the floor it was inaccessible for maintenance, that it caused noise and vibration below the passengers in the centre of the body, and that the frame height had to be about 3 ft. 2 in. laden above the ground, making entrance and exit difficult. The Foden rear-engined bus had a frame height of 2 ft. 7¾ in. laden, up to the rear axle, and 2 ft. 10½ in. behind it. Using the space at the rear of the frame enabled the engine to be transversely under the rear seats without loss of passenger space, and yet still vertical. All the vital parts of the engine and clutch, were immediately accessible through doors at the rear.

The wheelbase of 16 ft. 6 in. on the 30 ft. long rear-engined home Foden, and 19 ft. 6 in. on the 33-ft. export model, was chosen to give equal tyre loading, with the same tyres on all wheels; it also left sufficient length for a front entrance if desired. Both sides of the frame were kept completely clear of obstructions, so as to give more luggage-locker space than in the usual rear locker. Both 7 ft. 6 in. and 8 ft. widths were available, with right- or

An A.E.C. Regent Mark V of 1955 in the fleet of West Bridgford Urban District Council, in 1959, in the centre of Nottingham on the through service worked jointly by the West Bridgford and Nottingham municipalities.

An A.E.C. Regal Mark III 0962 single-decker of 1949, with Weymann bodywork, in service with the Midland General Omnibus Co. Ltd, standing outside Alfreton garage in 1962.

left-hand steering. Normally the Foden two-stroke engine was fitted, as chassis model "PVRF6", but the Gardner 6LW could also be used, as "PVRG6". Seating was normally for 43, as compared with 39 for the PVFE6. The radiator, quite a large one, was at the extreme rear end of the off-side, with a very large fan. Instead, therefore, of the usual distinctive Foden grille at the front end there was a full-width plain panel with, usually, a large diamond-shaped motif. The clutch was of orthodox single-plate type, quite close to the radiator, but the gearbox was mounted at an $83^{\circ}$ angle to it, with spiral bevel gears between them, and inclined downwards at about a $5^{\circ}$ angle. A very short propeller shaft took the drive from here to the under-slung-worm differential, which was near the off-side end of the axle instead of the far more usual near-side location.

With two such valuable contributions to bus design progress, in the first two-stroke engine and the first rear-engined chassis, it is a great pity that soon after the company's centenary celebration in summer 1956, Foden ceased making bus chassis and concentrated on heavy lorries. Between 1933 and 1956, Foden made a total of 582 buses and coaches, of which 101 were exported.

*Above* The Foden single-decker of 1945-56 had the same front-end treatment as the double-decker, with the bonnet sweeping across to cover the wing. This one has Windover bodywork, and ran for Biss Brothers, of Bishops Stortford, Hertfordshire, and was seen in 1955 at Clacton.

*Below left* Foden made this double-deck bus chassis in 1945-56, and sold quite a lot. Here in 1956 we see one with Northern Counties bodywork, owned by the Lancashire United Transport Ltd of Atherton, at the Punch Bowl, Atherton.

*Below right* The Foden rear-engined single-decker of 1950-56 had Foden's own unique two-stroke oil engine tucked away in the rear luggage locker. This one also had an unusual Whitson 1½-deck body, and was owned by Salopia Saloon Coaches Ltd of Whitchurch, Shropshire, as seen in 1959.

# FORD

*(Dagenham, Essex)*

Ford small 14-seat bus chassis had been made and sold quite extensively during 1923-32, being basically similar to Ford lorry chassis, but psv work had been dropped from 1933. Their buses and coaches did not reappear until early in 1960, and they can now be seen in all parts of Britain.

The Ford "Thames Trader" psv chassis of 1960 had a 17 ft. 8 in. wheelbase for 30 ft. × 7 ft. 6 in. bodywork and up to 41 seats. The engine could be either the Ford six-cylinder 4.89-litre petrol engine or the Ford six-cylinder 5.42-litre diesel, both of which were already well established in Thames Trader lorries. The frame was short and straight, cut off immediately behind the rear axle, leaving the body structure to support the load. In general appearance and layout the whole chassis was very similar to the Bedford SB, as also was the frontal appearance and the bodywork supplied for it by Duple, Plaxton, Harrington, Burlingham, and Yeates, who in each case had their own standard design which would fit either chassis. Indeed following the demise of most other makes of lightweight 41-seaters of orthodox front-engine layout these two were now the only serious rivals.

In September 1964, a 36-ft. long version of the same chassis appeared, known as the "Thames '36' P.S.V.", and seating 52. It used the same two engines, and other components. The extra length was gained by an 18 ft. 2 in. wheelbase and by mounting the engine well in front of the front wheels on a long forward extension of the main frame. The passenger entrance was also forward of the front wheels, which was not possible on the 30 ft. version. These two models lasted until early 1966, when they were replaced by the "R192" and "R226", with 16 ft. and 18 ft. 10 in. wheelbase, petrol or diesel in both cases.

In the early post-war vehicle shortage some operators had passenger bodywork built onto standard Ford Thames goods chassis, such as this one of H. S. Neave & Son, of Catfield, Norfolk, with Thurgood bodywork. It was seen in 1953 at the Potter Street Inn, near Epping.

Ford Thames did not make a proper psv chassis until 1960, but it then quickly became very popular. This one seen in 1963 was owned by S. A. Bebb Ltd of Llantwit Fardre, near Pontypridd, Glamorgan. The Duple bodywork was a standard design used also on some Bedford and Commer chassis, with almost the same frontal treatment.

A Bristol Lodekka LD6G of 1957, of the Southern Vectis Omnibus Co. Ltd, parked on Ryde Esplanade, Isle of Wight. This had an E.C.W. body, and was a standard type used by all the Tilling companies.

Three buses of Mid-Wales Motorways parked at Welshpool in 1962. They are a Bedford OB with the Mark II service-bus body, a single-deck Guy Arab with the lower type of radiator, and a chassisless Sentinel-Beadle STC 4/40.

# GUY

*(Wolverhampton, Staffordshire)*

In 1942, after three years of desperate wartime shortages, the Government asked Guy to make buses again, so the "Arab" or "FD" double-decker that had been dropped in 1934 was revived. The first one was finished in August, and went to Swindon. Only fifteen months later a ceremony marked the completion of the 1,000th wartime Arab, which went to Burton-on-Trent, and in December 1944 the 2,000th was completed. The Arab was a straightforward simple 56-seater, very typical of most buses of the early thirties, with the gearbox independently mounted amidships. The new Arab had a 16 ft. 3 in. wheelbase (4½ in. less than in 1934), the transmission line was moved to the near-side, and all aluminium castings had to be replaced by iron or steel. This increased the weight by 18½%, which, with full wartime loads of standing passengers, made the bus too heavy for the Gardner 5LW engine with which it was fitted. This had been foreseen, but production capacity was not then available for many 6LW engines.

Of the first 500 Arabs made about 40 were fitted with 6LW engines. On these 40, in order to standardise chassis and body details, the radiators were moved 6 in. forward. When supplies of the 6LW became easier, the Ministry of Supply allocated to each purchaser either an Arab five-cylinder for flat country or a six-cylinder engine for hilly areas. From the 501st Arab onwards ("Arab Mark 2") all radiators were mounted 6 in. forward, leaving a large gap between the radiator and the front of the engine on the 5LW models; the front wings swept forward with a reverse curve instead of finishing plain. Overall length was 26 ft. 5 in., some 5 in. more than the legal maximum at that time, so the Ministry granted special dispensation for these, the longest four-wheel double-deckers ever yet made for British use.

Being further forward as well as rather high the radiator hampered the driver's vision, so in 1947 in the "Arab Mark 3" the radiator and bonnet were dropped 4 in. lower down. The Mark 3's radiator was unaltered although from 1946 it was in polished aluminium instead of painted cast iron. Under licence from Park Royal, in 1947 Guy started to build bus bodywork for highbridge double-deckers. Many other minor improvements were made to the Arab. Most now had 6LW engines, a few still the 5LW, and in 1948-52 the huge 10.35-litre Meadows 6DC.630 six-cylinder oiler was also available. Westinghouse air brakes were available from 1946 as an alternative to vacuum-servo.

A single-deck Arab, to seat 34 on a 17 ft. 6 in. wheelbase, was also made from March 1946 to 1953, with the same improvements and alternative engines as above. This had the low radiator a year before the double-deckers. A Guy version of the fluid flywheel and epicyclic Wilson gearbox so long favoured by Daimler and A.E.C. came onto the market in 1949 and proved very popular. From 1948 an export single-deck Arab with 19 ft. 6 in. wheelbase was also made. In 1951 Birmingham Corporation introduced a new frontal grille for its own Guys, to cover the radiator and blend in with the bonnet and near-side wing. This was later adopted by Guy Motors on a new "Arab Mark 4" of 16 ft. 4 in. wheelbase for the 27 ft. overall length now permissible. When the grille was used the radiator was a plain block of tubes without the outer shell, but some Arab 4s did still have the visible radiator. From 1950, the home single-decker was also lengthened to have 18 ft. 5 in. wheelbase for 30 ft. overall length. A new 22 ft. wheelbase 36 ft. long export model was added in 1956, also a 30 ft. home double-decker with 18 ft. 6 in. wheelbase. All the various Arabs were available for most of the time in both 7 ft. 6 in. and 8 ft. widths, except these last two, which were 8 ft. only; the single-deckers were not made after 1959.

Like many other firms, Guy in September 1950 introduced an underfloor-engined single-decker, still named "Arab". This could have either 16 ft. 4 in. or 17 ft. 6 in. wheelbase for 30 ft. or 33 ft. overall length, with either 7 ft. 6 in. or 8 ft. width. The engine was the horizontal Gardner, either 5HLW or 6HLW. Either the Wilson or a constant-mesh gearbox could be fitted. The radiator was still at the front in the traditional position. A lightweight version of this chassis appeared in 1953, again like many other firms. This version had the same engines and main dimensions, but a frame of slightly smaller section, a hypoid rear axle instead of worm, a radiator amidships by the engine, and smaller tyres. An 18 ft. wheelbase 36 ft. long export version was added in 1957, but all three lengths vanished after 1959.

A really large single-deck chassis introduced in January 1958 was the Guy "Victory", intended mainly for export. With an 18 ft. wheelbase and a long overhang at each end it was 36 ft. long and 8 ft. 2½ in. wide. In certain countries where regulations permitted, it could have as many as 63 seats. The Gardner 6HLW engine was mounted horizontally, under the floor mid-way between the axles, and there was a choice of six different gearboxes, with a spiral-bevel rear axle and Bendix-Westinghouse air brakes. By the end of 1959 the Meadows HDC.500 and the Leyland 0.680 were available as alternative engines, and there was also a new "Victory Airide" chassis. This had the same main dimensions and transmission units, and the 0.680 engine, but instead of semi-elliptic springs it had air suspension on all four wheels, which reduced the frame height (laden) from 36 in. to 33 in. From 1961 there was also a 20 ft. 6 in. wheelbase version of the Airide for a 39 ft. overall length; both Airide models had disc brakes. The Victory range, for export only, is still being made today.

In the smaller types of chassis the pre-war "Wolf" and "Vixen" re-appeared in 1948 with, respectively, normal and forward control, up to 20 and 30 seats, wheelbases of 13 ft. and 14 ft. 9 in., overall lengths of 20 ft. and 26 ft., and the Guy 3.3- and 3.7-litre four-cylinder petrol engines. Both remained until 1956. A new "Otter" was added in September 1949, with either the Guy 3.7-litre petrol engine or the Gardner 4LK diesel. It was almost identical with the Vixen but with a slightly longer rear overhang, larger tyres, and slightly heavier. Otters were built individually, and not mass-produced. From January 1952 the Perkins P6(V) oil engine could also be fitted, as could a two-speed rear axle. From 1958 a third alternative engine was the B.M.C. 5.1-litre diesel. In 1953 to the special order of London Transport 84 Otters were supplied with P6(V) engine, and normal instead of forward control, incorporating the Ford Thames bonnet and frontal structure. All Otters vanished in 1960.

To replace the Vixen a somewhat heavier "Warrior" was introduced in September 1956, with 18 ft. 2 in. wheelbase for up to 42 seats, and the Meadows 5.43-litre vertical oil engine. At the same time there also appeared a new lightweight underfloor-engined "Warrior L.U.F.", using the horizontal version of the same engine mounted amidships, and of 16 ft. 4 in. wheelbase. The frame was cropped short at both ends, leaving the body structure to make up the 30 ft. length. From 1957 the vertical Warrior could also have the 4LW Gardner engine, and the horizontal 5HLW; from September 1958 the A.E.C. 7.7-litre oiler was available for both Warrior and L.U.F., as were the B.M.C. 5.1-litre and the Leyland 0.370 engines a year later. This gave a choice of five makes of engine for the one chassis. The vertical Warrior (in Mark II form) was made until 1966, but the L.U.F. version vanished in 1961.

Guy's most spectacular chassis was "Wulfrunian", an entirely new double-decker introduced at the end of 1959, and which they advertised as "the most advanced passenger vehicle in the world". It had air suspension for both axles instead of leaf springing; its very low chassis (only 18 in. above ground) and low floor level brought the overall height down to only 13 ft. 3½ in., and yet it was a 78-seater with a conventional body floor design. The chassis was intended for integral construction with the body. The entrance was forward of the front axle, as was the engine, mounted vertically and to the off-side of the centre, so the driver was squeezed over to the extreme right-hand side and very cramped. The staircase was on the front near-side, with its base very close to the doorway, rising towards the rear and above the near-side front wheel. The wheelbase was only 15 ft. 4 in. for the 30 ft. × 8 ft. length and width. Three alternative engines were available: the Gardner 6LW and 6LX and the Leyland 0.600. The gearbox was a special one, wide and flat, under the floor and below the 18-in. frame height. Altogether it was a most unusual chassis, quite different from any other, the world's first bus with both air springs and disc brakes. A 17 ft. wheelbase version for rear-entrance bodywork with the three different engines was also available from 1959, but a year later this was dropped and replaced by 16 ft. 2 in. and 18 ft. alternatives. Both of these, and also the front-entrance version, remained on the market until 1965, but the Wulfrunian had not been as successful as Guy had hoped. The West Riding fleet at Wakefield bought a large quantity, but

A Daimler CVG6 of 1956, with ornamental front grille and concealed radiator, and with East Lancashire bodywork, at Cardiff bus station in 1959 on a local city route of Cardiff Corporation Transport.

One of a large fleet of Guy Wulfrunian chassisless integral double-deckers of 1959-62 purchased by the West Riding Automobile Co. Ltd, of Wakefield, Yorkshire. It had a Roe body, and was photographed in 1969.

only a handful were sold elsewhere, and these did not remain in service very long.

Guy reluctantly went back to the Arab. The "Arab Mark V", which appeared in autumn 1962, had a frame height 2½ in. lower than previously (only 21½ in.). Although the rear of the chassis frame was chopped off at only 25 ft. 5½ in., the 18 ft. 6 in. wheelbase for 30 ft. bodywork left the body structure to support the load. The traditional front vertical engine and half-width cab with bulkhead were used, with an improved panelling design blending the cab into the near-side wing and bonnet. The entrance and stairs could be at either front or rear. The engine was the 6LW. A 16 ft. 4 in. wheelbase model for 27 ft. bodywork was also offered, and both models were on sale for about ten years.

Unfortunately the Guy business was purchased in 1962 by Jaguar, which already owned Daimler, so after a few years it was decided to phase out buses and leave Guy to concentrate on heavy lorries.

*Above* Guy Arabs were almost the only double-deckers allowed to be made during the war. The first 500, of 1942-3, had the Gardner 5LW engine and a high radiator and bonnet. This one, of F. J. Honeywood, of Stanstead, Suffolk, is seen in 1953 at Bury St Edmunds, and has Park Royal utility bodywork.

The Guy Arab of 1943-7 had the radiator mounted further forward, leaving enough space for a 6LW engine, and had a longer bonnet, and wings curling forwards. Here is one with Roe bodywork and owned by the West Riding Automobile Co. Ltd, of Wakefield, parked in 1957 in Leeds bus station.

The Guy Arab Mark 3 of 1947-51 had the radiator and bonnet dropped lower down, but the engine, and the access holes in the bonnet side, stayed at their former level. Here in 1954 is one with Park Royal bodywork owned by Southampton Corporation pausing at the Royal Pier.

*Above left* The Guy Arab Mark 3 appeared also in single-deck form in 1946-53. This one of Moore Brothers (Kelvedon) Ltd, Essex, has Strachan bodywork, and is standing in Chelmsford bus station in 1963.

*Above right* Here in 1962 is the Guy Arab Mark 4 of 1951-60 with Strachan bodywork, owned by Graham's Bus Service, of Paisley, Renfrewshire.

*Left* The underfloor-engined single-deck Guy Arab was made in 1950-59. Here in 1963 is one with Alexander body owned by the Western S.M.T. Co. Ltd, standing outside the John O' Groats Hotel, north Scotland

A long-wheelbase Leyland Titan PD3/4 of 1957, with a Metro-Cammell body, owned by J. James & Sons Ltd of Ammanford, Carmarthenshire, seen in 1959 at the Ammanford bus terminus near the county school.

A Leyland Titan PD2/12 of 1951, with Weymann bodywork, in the fleet of Wallasey Corporation, Cheshire, waiting in 1962 at the Seacombe ferry terminus to connect with the arrival of the ferry boat from Liverpool.

The Guy Vixen of 1948-56 was a much smaller chassis, of orthodox layout. Here in 1953 is one with Wadham bodywork owned by the West Wight Motor Bus Co. Ltd, Totland Bay, Isle of Wight. The Otter was almost identical in appearance, and the Wolf was the same but shorter.

The Guy Wulfrunian of 1959-64 was a most ingenious vehicle with many unique features. Almost all of them were sold in Yorkshire; one of the very few elsewhere was owned by West Wales Motors Ltd, of Ammanford, Carmarthenshire, seen here with East Lancashire bodywork in 1961. Note the very low overall height and floor height.

The Guy Arab Mark V of 1962-72 had many detail improvements over the Mark 4, and another new radiator and frontal design. Here in 1963 is one of a batch bought by Wolverhampton Corporation, the long-wheelbase version. It has bodywork by Metro-Cammell.

# JENSEN

*(West Bromwich, Staffordshire)*

For many years the law restricted goods vehicles of more than 2½ tons unladen weight to a maximum speed of only 20 mph, but those of less than 2½ tons were allowed to do 30 mph. This took no account of the payload carried, and thus created the absurd situation (from the road safety point of view) where a vehicle weighing 49½ cwt empty and carrying a five-ton load was allowed to travel half as fast again as one weighing 51 cwt but unladen. The 50 cwt limit had to be the total weight of chassis plus bodywork. Both chassis and body builders adopted all sorts of ingenious methods for making the vehicles lighter, and yet strong enough to carry heavier and heavier loads.

Jensen was the only firm to make a chassisless integral lorry all in one, and at the same time to use lightweight aluminium alloy throughout. They thus managed to produce a large full-sized covered van weighing just 50 cwt, the total of "chassis" plus body, and yet capable of carrying six tons of useful load. It was terribly expensive, being almost entirely aluminium, but plenty of operators thought it was well worth the cost, being allowed to run at 30 mph, and so during about 1946 and 1960 they could be seen all over Britain.

Following this success Jensen modified the design to make the "JNSN" 40-seat bus or coach chassis, which was first seen in November 1948, with a 16 ft. 2 in. wheelbase and 27 ft. × 7 ft. 5 in. length and width, weighing only 2 tons 12 cwt. It was based largely on tubular framing, with the Perkins P6(V) engine mounted vertically at the front. Bodywork was made by Sparshatt of Portsmouth or A.C.B. of Sunderland, and the complete vehicle plus 40 passengers weighed only 7 tons 10 cwt. The JNSN coach was very silent and smooth-running; it could climb a hill of 1-in-3, and gave a fuel consumption in average conditions of 17¾ mpg.

When the 20 mph speed limit for heavy goods vehicles was abolished in 1951, Jensen's main market was totally destroyed for nobody was prepared to buy an expensive all-aluminium lorry now that a heavier but cheaper steel one was allowed to run faster. As several other firms had recently started to make chassisless integral buses, it was not economic for Jensen to continue with their own, so this vanished in 1952. A few had been sold to various operators. Jensen reverted to building goods bodywork only, and although they did produce another lightweight van chassis (a small 25-cwt one) in 1958 they never again tried buses or coaches.

The Jensen coach was made in 1948-52. This one, with Reading & Co. bodywork, was bought new by E. H. Crinage & Son, Ventnor, Isle of Wight, and later sold to A. H. Fluck, of Stow-on-the-Wold, Gloucestershire.

A Leyland-Metro-Cammell Olympic chassisless single-decker of Ribble Motor Services Ltd, Preston, dating from 1951 and using Royal Tiger units, seen in 1962 in the village of Cartmel in the far north of Lancashire.

A lightweight Leyland-Metro-Cammell chassisless Olympian of the Western Welsh Omnibus Co. Ltd, made in 1956 and using Tiger Cub units, is seen in 1959 at the Llanelly bus terminus.

# KARRIER

*(Luton, Bedfordshire)*

Karrier was an important maker of heavier types of buses and lorries until 1934 when the firm was sold to Rootes and the Huddersfield factory was closed. In September 1952, Karrier re-entered the bus field, though only as a small shadow of its former self. Advertised as "A Rootes Product", but under the name of "Karrier", and made by Karrier Motors Ltd of Luton, Beds, there appeared a new small 14-seat forward-control psv coach chassis with 10 ft. 3 in. wheelbase and 16 ft. 6 in. overall length. The engine was the Commer four-cylinder side-valve petrol unit of 2¼ litres. The bodies were made by Reading & Co. Ltd, of Portsmouth, in conjunction with Karrier, with 14 luxury coach seats spaced two on one side of the gangway and only one on the other, the width being only 6 ft. 9 in.

Early in 1960 an alternative oil engine became available, in the Standard four-cylinder 2¼-litre unit, and a new 12-seat bus body was introduced by B. Walker & Son Ltd, of Watford, Herts. Both engines and both bodies remained in production until 1964, when the chassis was withdrawn and Karrier again vanished from the bus world, though it still exists making refuse-collection and gully-emptying vehicles as part of the Dodge/Commer/Karrier division of Chrysler U.K. Ltd.

The Karrier 14-seater of 1952-64, with Reading bodywork, in the Caerphilly Greys fleet of Ivor Pursey, of Caerphilly, Glamorganshire, is seen here in 1963 standing outside his garage.

# LEYLAND

*(Leyland, Lancashire)*

After the war a Leyland range appeared quite different from pre-war except in the basic orthodox layout. This used a new 7.4-litre oil engine which Leyland developed early in the war for army lorries. The "PD1" or "Titan" double-deck bus with 16 ft. 3 in. wheelbase was announced in September 1945, and by December 52 operators had ordered it. It went into production from January 1946, and gave a fuel consumption of 14 mpg at its top speed of 39 mph. But the PD1 did not last long, as the 7.4-litre engine was not powerful enough, and its main rivals were already larger, as also was the pre-war Leyland oil engine.

In June 1946 it was announced that a new 0.600 oil engine of 9.8 litres was soon to go into production, and that it would require no more fuel than the 7.4. In May 1947 a new "PD2" chassis was announced, using this engine, and with a new synchromesh gearbox, the first heavy-duty one on the British market. The PD2 became one of the most successful British bus designs ever, and many thousands were made over the next 22 years. Variations in 1947 were: "PD2/1" with 16 ft. 3 in. wheelbase for 26 ft. × 7 ft. 6 in. length and width; "PD2/3" the same but 8 ft. wide; and "OPD2/1" with 17 ft. 6 in. wheelbase for overseas 27 ft. 6 in. × 8 ft. bodywork. Five PD1s to these larger dimensions, and seating 66 instead of 56, had recently entered service in Dublin, Ireland, as a foretaste of what was not yet allowed in Britain but soon would be. As soon as the 27 ft. length was allowed in Britain, from 1 June 1950 onwards, Leyland increased the home PD2 wheelbase to 16 ft. 5 in., and produced the 7 ft. 6 in. wide "PD2/10" and "PD2/11" chassis with vacuum and air brakes respectively; also the 8 ft. wide "PD2/12" and "PD2/13" with vacuum and air brakes.

In 1954 the PD2/10, 11, 12 & 13 were re-designated as PD2/22, PD2/23, PD2/20, and PD2/21 respectively, but remained unchanged, with the dry-plate clutch and synchromesh gearbox. Two new models were also introduced: "PD2/24" and "PD2/25", respectively 8 ft. and 7 ft. 6 in. wide but with the same wheelbase and air brakes. These had a fluid coupling and Leyland's new "Pneumo-Cyclic" direct air-shift semi-automatic four-speed epicyclic gearbox, for two-pedal driving. Two further models introduced in 1954 were the special lightweight "PD2/26" and "PD2/27", with pneumo-cyclic and synchromesh gearboxes respectively. Both were 8 ft. wide with 16 ft. 5 in. wheelbase and air brakes, but had a lighter frame and springs, smaller tyres, rear axle, and fuel tank, and were to carry only lightweight bodywork.

All these models could have either an exposed polished radiator and half cab, or a new full-width grille concealing the radiator and blending into the bonnet and near-side wing. In 1955 all home models adopted the smaller rear axle with 8 in. worm centres instead of 9 in., and the separate lightweight models were dropped. The PD2/20, 21, 22, & 23 were then re-designated as PD2/30, PD2/27, PD2/31, and PD2/28 respectively. From then onwards the terms PD2/24 to 31 were used only for concealed-radiator models, and the same chassis with exposed radiators were known as "PD2/34" to "PD2/41" respectively. All 7 ft. 6 in. models were dropped from 1962, but the 8 ft. models (suffix 24, 27, 30, 34, 37, and 40) were still made until 1968.

Meanwhile the 30 ft. long "PD3" range on 18 ft. 6 in. wheelbase for home use was introduced in September 1956. These were the "PD3/1" and "PD3/4" with synchromesh gearbox and air brakes; "PD3/2" and "PD3/5" pneumo-cyclic and air; and "PD3/3" and "PD3/6" with synchromesh and vacuum. Stroke 1, 2, and 3 had concealed radiators, and 4, 5, and 6 were exposed. All were 8 ft. wide, with the same 0.600 engine and the larger rear axle with 9 in. centres for the underslung worm. The PD3/3 was dropped in 1962, but the other five continued unchanged until 1968.

Turning to single-deckers, the new "PS1" or "Tiger" appeared in early 1946, with 17 ft. 6 in. wheelbase and 27 ft. 6 in. overall length, and with the same improvements over the pre-war Tiger as had the Titan. The PS1 itself had a high straight frame extension behind the rear axle, and the "PS1/1" had a dropped extension suitable for rear-entrance bus work or a large luggage locker on a coach. Both were 7 ft. 6 in. wide. In May 1947, as with the Titans, the 7.4-litre engine was replaced by the new 9.8-litre unit, and the "PS2" range appeared, with the new synchromesh gearbox. The "PS2/1" and "PS2/3" were 7 ft. 6 in. wide with straight and dropped rear frame extension, and the "PS2/5" and "PS2/7" were 8 ft. wide with straight and dropped frame. For overseas there was a similar "OPS" range with 19 ft. and 21 ft. 6 in. wheelbases. For home use a larger 30 ft. × 8 ft. model on 18 ft. 9 in. wheelbase appeared in the summer of 1950, as "PS2/12" and "PS2/13" with straight and dropped frame. All home Tigers were discontinued from 1953, but the overseas range lasted until 1968.

A horizontal version of the 9.8-litre 0.600 engine appeared in October 1948, with an overall height of only 22 in.; all accessories were arranged for easy reach from outside an underfloor-engined bus. It was used first in the Olympic (see later). In April 1950 the new "Royal Tiger" appeared, to replace the PS2. This was a heavyweight chassis 30 ft. long with 15 ft. 7 in. wheelbase for 44 seats. With 7 ft. 6 in. width there were the "PSU1/9" with vacuum brakes and "PSU1/10" with air brakes, both with full-length straight frame for bus work; also the "PSU1/11" and "PSU1/12" with vacuum and air brakes and the frame cut short behind the rear axle to allow for coaches whose body framing would support a large low luggage locker. Similarly with 8 ft. width there were the "PSU1/13" and "PSU1/14" with vacuum and air brakes and long rear frame; and the "PSU1/15" and "PSU1/16" with vacuum and air brakes and short rear frame. These frame differences were to accommodate different entrance positions, and involved different locations for fuel tank, battery, and spare wheel. The main part of all the frames was straight save for only a very small rear wheelarch. For overseas there was a range of 17 ft. 6 in. and 20 ft. 4 in. wheelbase "OPSU" Royal Tigers with long and short rear frames.

The Royal Tiger was well received, and within only five months 200 operators all over the world had placed large orders, several for more than 100 vehicles. By four years later Leyland had already made 6,000 underfloor-engined buses. From April 1954 the larger 11.1-litre 0.680 horizontal engine was fitted, as was a pneumo-cyclic gearbox – mounted remote from the engine, a new underslung-worm rear axle, and improved diaphragm-operated air brakes. The name "Royal Tiger World-master" was adopted. The 30 ft. × 8 ft. home model was increased to 16 ft. 3 in. wheelbase and redesignated "RT3/1" and "RT3/2" with and without frame extension, but the 11-litre engine was too big for British operators, most of whom bought the new Tiger Cub instead. The R.T.W. overseas chassis now had two alternative frame heights, and had either 18 ft. or 20 ft. wheelbase; they are still in production.

In 1950 the trend was towards chassisless integral construction where the body was built with a much stronger underframe, directly to support the mechanical units without a separate chassis. Six other firms tried this method around then, and in February Leyland Motors, in conjunction with Metropolitan-Cammell-Weymann Ltd, jointly announced their new "Olympic". This was a chassisless version of the Royal Tiger, with the same 0.600 engine, gearbox, axles, braking, etc. Prototypes had been running in several areas for 18 months, and production was now well under way. M.C.W. had built other chassisless vehicles back in 1936, and was a pioneer of all-metal bodywork in 1931.

Four sizes of Olympic were now available. The home model, "HR40", had 15 ft. 7 in. wheelbase for 27 ft. 6 in. length and 40 seats at either 7 ft. 6 in. or 8 ft. width. For export there were 15 ft. 1 in., 17 ft. 6 in., and 20 ft. 4 in. wheelbase versions, and already 50 had been ordered for Uruguay. Later in 1950 another home model, the "HR44" with 15 ft. 7 in. wheelbase for 30 ft. length and 44 seats, at either width, was introduced. The bodywork of all models was of high-grade steel, and the longitudinal load-carrying members extended from the floorline to the waistline. Home Olympics had a doorway forward of the front axle, but export models had two doors, one in front of each axle. The Olympic was extremely silent, with no noise inside from the engine or gearbox. It gave 11.6 mpg at 40 mph, and 9.1 mpg on bus work with five stops per mile. All five Olympics remained on the market until 1956.

Experience with the Royal Tiger proved it was heavier than necessary so in September 1952 a lightweight underfloor-engined "Tiger Cub" was introduced. This had a horizontal version of the 5.76-litre 0.350 engine previously used in Leyland Comets. The Tiger Cub chassis weighed only 3¾ tons, and gave 16 mpg for fuel on straight-run tests. The original model was the

"PSUC1/1", for bus use only, and it had 16 ft. 2 in. wheelbase for 44 seats for 30 ft. × 8 ft. A year later a coach version, the "PSUC1/2", was introduced, in which the rear end of the frame was cut short, and the 0.350 engine was up-rated to give 108 bhp instead of 90. In September 1954 a "PSUC1/3" bus was added, with single-speed rear axle and the hydraulic coupling and pneumocyclic gearbox instead of dry-plate clutch and constant-mesh box. For overseas there were eight models in the "OPSUC" range. For home use 7 ft. 6 in. versions were not made until October 1956; they were the "PSUC1/4" pneumo-cyclic and "PSUC1/5" with constant mesh. From February 1962 Tiger Cubs had the larger 0.400 engine instead of 0.350, the model numbers being all increased by /10, thus PSUC1/3 became PSUC1/13, etc. They remained on the market until 1969.

A chassisless integral version of the Tiger Cub, known as "Olympian", was introduced jointly by M.C.W. and Leyland in September 1953. It was a lightweight version of the Olympic, and weighed 5¼ tons empty. The wheelbase was 16 ft. 2 in., the same as the Tiger Cub, and the engine and all mechanical units were the same as on the original PSUC1/1. It lasted only three years and vanished in 1956.

Despite dropping the 9.8-litre engine from the Royal Tiger in 1954 in favour of the larger Worldmaster and the smaller Tiger Cub, it was found there was still a need for it, so the 9.8 was used in a new "Leopard" underfloor-engined 30 ft.×8 ft. single-decker which appeared at the end of 1959. Apart from the engine the rest of the chassis was mostly the same as the Tiger Cub, with 16 ft. 2 in. wheelbase. The "L1" had a straight rear frame extension for bus work, and the "L2" a dropped extension for coaching. A 36 ft. long Leopard with 18 ft. 6 in. wheelbase was added in October 1961; it was known as "PSU3/1", and had synchromesh gearbox and straight frame extension. Three other 18 ft. 6 in. models were added in May 1963; "PSU3/2" with fluid coupling and pneumo-cyclic gearbox and straight frame extension; "PSU3/3" (synchromesh and dropped frame); and "PSU3/4" (pneumo-cyclic and dropped frame). In September 1965 the L1 and L2 were re-designated "PSU4/1" and "PSU4/3", and two new 16 ft. 2 in. pneumo-cyclic models "PSU4/2" and "PSU4/4" were added with straight and dropped frame extensions. The Leopard has proved very popular, and is now widely used throughout most of Britain, and is still on sale.

Returning to 1949, nothing had yet replaced the small pre-war 26-seat Leyland Cub or the lightweight Cheetah, so in July a new home "Comet" appeared. This was a normal-control bonneted chassis on 17 ft. 6 in. wheelbase, 27 ft. long, and could seat up to 33, in both 7 ft. 6 in. and 8 ft. widths. The "CPP1" had a 5-litre Leyland petrol engine, and the "CPO1" a new but very similar 5-litre Leyland oil engine, the 0.300, which had first appeared in February 1948 with the export Comet. The engine mounting was unusual, with four rubber-bushed link shackles. In October 1952 the home Comets were radically altered, as "Comet 90", and upgraded to forward-control with full-width cab and no separate bulkhead. The larger 90 bhp 0.350 engine was fitted instead of 0.300, a new gearbox was used, and there were now two alternative wheelbases, 16 ft. 11 in. ("ECPO2/1") for 27 ft. 6 in. bodywork, and 14 ft. 8 in. ("ECPO2/2") for 25 ft. length. From 1962 a still larger engine, the 0.370, was used, and Comets are still made today.

After some months of rumours, and secret trials with Ribble, the first prototype rear-engined double-decker was announced in October 1954. This bus had an ordinary rear entrance, and the rather small 0.350 Comet 90 engine mounted vertically and transversely on the platform behind this, with a turbo-charger to increase its horse-power from 90 to 150, and a radiator behind a grille on the off-side of the bodywork. The drive was through a fluid coupling and Wilson four-speed gearbox to an angle drive on the off-side and a spiral-bevel gear to an underslung axle. To obtain a low floor level the height of the axle was reduced by using hub-reduction gears. Rear suspension was by coil springs so large that seats could not be placed over the wheelarches; therefore this space, also the top of the engine, was available for luggage. Independent front suspension was used. The platform and saloon floor level were only 18½ in. above ground, but the cab floor was 12 in. above this, and access for the driver was by a sliding door in the bulkhead instead of from outside. Seating was for 61. The second prototype, a year later, was the same size and layout, but had only a half-width instead of full-width cab. Frontal treatment was very similar to the 1938-9 TF and CR types – again with driver access from the saloon, which at that time was unique for a double-decker.

The production "Atlantean" was announced in September 1956. It was a much bigger bus, seating 78 in the 30 ft. × 8 ft. box dimensions, with a long front overhang and a 16 ft. 3 in. wheelbase that was less than the 27 ft. PD2 Titan which claimed to be far more manoeuvrable. The Comet engine was now much too small, so the 0.600 was used (the same as the PD2). It was still mounted vertically and transversely at the rear, but needed far more space so the entrance was moved to the front, in front of the axle and alongside the driver. The floor level was only 17½ in. and overall height was 13 ft. 3 in., about a foot less than most ordinary double-deckers, whilst still retaining a central gangway upstairs. The engine exhaust was discharged at roof height, as an anti-pollution feature. The bodywork of semi-integral all-metal construction, with body pillars permanently fixed to the chassis, was designed as a complete unit by Leyland, although several other firms built it.

After two years the idea of a completely integrated structure was abandoned in favour of a separate self-contained chassis frame, giving greater freedom of design to the bodybuilder, and the original built-in heating and ventilating system was discarded. Conventional semi-elliptic front and rear springs were now fitted instead of independent suspension, and a more orthodox rear axle was used. Its 78 seats and a flat floor upstairs now increased the height to 14 ft. 1 in., giving trouble with some railway bridges, though a lower height was possible with only 73 seats and a two-level floor with side gangway at the rear end upstairs. In this revised form the Atlantean "PDR1/1" became a best-seller, and still is. Well over 2,000 had been sold in Britain by May 1964, when a revised form of dropped-centre stepped double-reduction rear axle was re-introduced as an alternative, as the "PDR1/2".

The Leyland Titan PD1 of 1945-6 had a 7.4-litre engine. Some of them also had bodywork by Leyland, as did this one of the King Alfred Motor Services of R. Chisnell & Sons Ltd, Winchester, Hampshire, seen in 1953.

The Leyland Titan PD2 of 1947-68 in various forms had the larger 9.8-litre engine. This one, of the PD2/10 sub-type seen in 1953, has the longer wheelbase of 1950 onwards. Also in the King Alfred fleet, it shows the improvements made to Leyland bodywork before bodybuilding ceased in 1954.

The 8 ft. wide PD2/37 version of the Titan PD2 is seen here in 1960 with Massey Bros body and in the fleet of Baxter's Bus Services Ltd of Airdrie, Lanarkshire.

### *Leyland*

From 1955 all Titans could optionally have the radiator hidden behind a grille (as shown here in 1956), with the bonnet sweeping across to cover the wing as Foden did in 1945. This one, with East Lancs bodywork, was owned by Leigh Corporation in Lancashire.

The 30 ft. long PD3 Leyland Titan appeared in 1956. The PD3/1 version shown here in 1975 had a new design of fibreglass frontal treatment which could also be used on PD2s; the exposed radiator or 1955 style of grille could be used on PD3s. This bus, with Park Royal bodywork, was owned by Leicester Corporation.

The Leyland Tiger PS1 of 1946-7 with smaller engine, and the PS2 family of 1947-53 with larger engine, had the same radiator and bonnet as the PD1 and earlier PD2s. This PS2/3 with Willowbrook body was owned by Stratford-upon-Avon Blue Motors Ltd, and was seen in 1960.

The Leyland Royal Tiger of 1950-54, like most other underfloor-engined single-deckers, had most of its identifiable features hidden by the body. This one, with Metalcraft body, was owned in 1959 by Buckmaster Garages Ltd of Leighton Buzzard, Bedfordshire.

This chassisless underfloor-engined Leyland Olympic of 1950-56, made jointly with Metro-Cammell, was acquired by B. K. Jennings, of Ashen, near Sudbury, Suffolk, and is seen here in 1953 at his garage.

*Left* The lightweight underfloor-engined Leyland Tiger Cub, with a smaller engine than the Royal Tiger, was made in 1952–69. Here is an early example, of Hall Bros (South Shields) Ltd with Strachan bodywork, seen in 1957 at Doncaster Waterdales bus station.

*Below* The bonneted version of the Leyland Comet was made in 1949-52, though later Comets had forward control. This one, with Strachan body, was bought by F. A. Flin, of Croydon, and later sold to Chiltern Queens Ltd, of Woodcote, Oxfordshire, where it is seen in 1957.

The first two prototype rear-engined Leyland double-deckers were basically a Titan PD2 chassis with a Comet engine transversely behind the rear entrance. The second of the two, seen here in 1959, had a frontal treatment like the pre-war CR and TF types, and was sold to Lowland Motorways Ltd of Shettleston, near Glasgow. Bodywork was by M.C.W.

After five years of development the standard production model of the Leyland Atlantean rear-engined double-decker from 1958 onwards was totally different from the prototypes. This one, with Roe bodywork and owned by Sheffield Corporation, is standing outside their Greenland Road garage in 1962.

In order to see how the engine was accommodated we must look at the rear end of the Leyland Atlantean in 1961. This one was owned by Silver Star Motor Services Ltd of Porton Down, near Salisbury, Wiltshire, and had Weymann bodywork.

# MAUDSLAY

*(Alcester, Warwickshire)*

At the end of the war a quick transition from tanks and aircraft work led to a new range of four-, six-, and eight-wheel lorries and luxury coach chassis being developed, and new machinery was installed in both the Coventry and the Alcester factories. The "Marathon Mark III" coach chassis was available by March 1946, with a 17 ft. 7 in. wheelbase and 27 ft. 6 in. × 7 ft. 6 in. layout that followed standard practice. It used the A.E.C. 7.7-litre oil engine, but de-rated to give only 98 bhp at 1800 rpm instead of 108 at 2000.

The "Marathon Mark II" chassis, with the same wheelbase and overall dimensions, was available by September 1946, using the Maudslay six-cylinder overhead-valve petrol engine, with a chassis weight of 3 tons 19 cwt. A 30 ft. × 8 ft. version of the 7.7-engined chassis, with 19 ft. 3 in. wheelbase, was made in the summer of 1950, legally usable from 1 June onwards. From March 1949 there was also an export Marathon Mark III with 17 ft. 7 in. or 20 ft. wheelbase, using the A.E.C. 9.6-litre engine.

Maudslay sold out to A.E.C. in 1949, and soon the Marathons ceased. But the name was kept alive. The Alcester factory was turned over to making axles and gearboxes for Southall, which it did for over 20 years. Southall-built Regal Mark III, Regal Mark IV, and Regent Mark III chassis, identical to the A.E.C. product save only for the name, were advertised as "Maudslay Marathon Mark IIIA", "Maudslay Marathon Mark IV", and "Maudslay Regent Mark III", even though Maudslay had never made an underfloor-engined chassis of its own and had not made any double-deckers for 18 years. Later the Reliance and Monocoach, and all the standard A.E.C. lorry types, were advertised under the Maudslay name, and this continued until 1959. A few lorries were sold thus, but no buses or coaches except nine "Maudslay" 9612E Regents which Coventry Corporation had ordered from A.E.C. in 1949 which were assembled at Alcester in 1951 on the "support home industry" principle.

Here in 1962 is a Maudslay Marathon of 1946-51 with Duple body owned by Creamline Motor Services (Bordon) Ltd of Bordon, Hampshire, at their garage. This Mark III had an A.E.C. 7.7 oil engine.

A few of the last Maudslays to be built, in 1950-51, were 8 ft. wide and did not have the standard radiator and bonnet. This one with Burlingham body was owned by Garelochhead Coach Services Ltd in Dunbartonshire, Scotland, as seen in 1963.

# MORRIS-COMMERCIAL

*(Adderley Park, Birmingham)*

From 1948 to 1952 Morris-Commercial made only one psv chassis. This was a lightweight, forward-control 32-seater with 14 ft. 11 in. wheelbase for 26 ft. overall length, of conventional layout, with no unusual features. This chassis first appeared in October 1948, with only an oil engine. This was a six-cylinder 4¼-litre unit made under licence from Adolphe Saurer, S.A., of Switzerland, to Saurer designs. The Nuffield Organisation had acquired the right to do this in 1938, but apart from a few prototypes in 1939 the war prevented any being made for ten years. Once in production it sold extensively in Morris-Commercial lorries, but not many buses or coaches were made. The compression ratio was much higher than on any other British bus engine, 19-to-1, all others ranging from 14 to 17, and at the top of the stroke each piston came much closer to the face of the cylinder head than usual. Fuel consumption averaged 20 mpg. In September 1950 this engine was enlarged to 4½ litres.

An alternative petrol engine became available in 1949, the two bus chassis thereafter being known as type "OP" (oil passenger) and type "PP" (petrol passenger). The petrol engine was a newly-designed Morris-Commercial unit of 3.77 litres with four cylinders, which, again, found far more use in goods vehicles. The Morris bus and coach chassis was directly competitive with the very similar Austin chassis. When the two firms amalgamated in 1952, surprisingly both ceased making psv chassis for home use and the new British Motor Corporation then kept solely to goods vehicles and private cars.

The Morris-Commercial PP and OP chassis, with Morris petrol and Saurer diesel engines, were made in 1948-52. Here in 1960 is an OP with Plaxton bodywork; it was owned by the Stag Garage Ltd of Lochgilphead, Argyllshire.

# ROWE

*(Liskeard, Cornwall)*

The Rowe chassis, which was announced to the press at the end of 1953, was designed to cope with steep hills, narrow roads, and sharp corners. It had a straight frame of conventional layout, with 17 ft. wheelbase and 28 ft. overall length, including a bolt-on dropped rear extension. A Meadows 4DC.330 oil engine was mounted vertically at the front. This chassis was able to start from rest, with a full load, on a 1-in-4 gradient, and yet reach a maximum speed of 56 mph. It was developed by a small Cornish independent bus operator, M. G. Rowe, who called it the "Hillmaster". By autumn 1954 he was also making and selling Hillmasters with a horizontal underfloor engine (the Meadows 4HDC.330) mounted amidships, a frame height of 36 in., 16 ft. 6 in. wheelbase and 30 ft. overall length, most of the other components being the same as before.

Also in 1954 Rowe started making a 7 ton lorry chassis, with the same vertical 4DC.330 engine. For several years both his passenger and his goods chassis sold quite well to small operators in Devon and Cornwall, but their influence further afield was limited. Most of the coaches had Whitson bodywork. In 1956 another Hillmaster coach chassis was marketed, with the larger 6HDC.500 oil engine horizontally under the floor; this had the same bore and stroke but six cylinders instead of four. The chassis was 8 ft. wide instead of 7 ft. 6 in., and had a two-speed rear axle, but was otherwise substantially the same. From 1957 onwards the Gardner 4HLW or the A.E.C. AH 410 engine were available as alternatives to the Meadows 330, and the Gardner 5HLW or 6HLW or the A.E.C. AH 470 as alternatives to the Meadows 500. Rowe chassis were not made after 1960, and the firm reverted to being only an operator.

The Rowe Hillmaster coach chassis was made in 1953-60 with both vertical front and underfloor horizontal engines, and eight different types of engine. They sold well to operators in Devon and Cornwall, and here we see one with vertical Meadows engine and Whitson bodywork at an exhibition in London in 1954, with one of the lorries which Rowe also made.

# RUTLAND

*(Addington, Surrey)*

The Rutland chassis was made by Motor Traction Ltd, of Addington, near Croydon, Surrey, which was founded in 1949. In its first five years Rutland built and sold a range of six lorry chassis from 3-tonners to 10-tonners, all of conventional layout. In July 1954, they entered the passenger market with a coach chassis of very unusual layout known as the Rutland "Clipper". This was for 30 ft. × 8 ft. bodywork, with a 16 ft. 6 in. wheelbase, and built mainly from well-proved proprietory components, which were assembled in unusual locations. The Perkins "R6(V)" oil engine was mounted at the rear, vertically, and in line with the chassis, so as to avoid any complicated bevel gearing in the transmission such as is necessary when a rear engine is mounted transversely. Rutland took the output shaft above the rear axle, and well forward of it, to a point half-way along the chassis where it entered a transfer gearbox, from which another shaft drove back again to the rear axle.

By July 1956 an alternative engine was available for the rear-engined chassis, i.e. the Meadows 4DC.330, and a horizontal underfloor-engined chassis was also now being offered, with six different alternative engines; Meadows 4HDC.330, the Gardner 4HLW, 5HLW, and 6HLW, and the A.E.C. AH 470 or AH 410. But Rutland and the M.T. Co. went out of business a few years later.

This Rutland Clipper rear-engined single-decker of 1958 has a Meadows engine and Whitson bodywork, and was owned by Acorn Motors Ltd of Hanworth, Middlesex.

# SEDDON

*(Oldham, Lancashire)*

Seddon chassis were not made until autumn 1948, when the passenger "Mark 4" appeared. (Marks 1, 2, and 3, also 5, 8, and 9, were goods vehicles). The Mark 4 was a 25 ft. long 32-seat bus or 28-seat coach with 14 ft. 11 in. wheelbase. Its designer took care to reduce the unladen weight to a minimum, and this was supported by excellent acceleration and fuel consumption, and the cost was reduced by the Seddon organisation having the lowest possible overheads.

As far as possible the chassis used existing well-known proprietory components. The engine was the famous 4¼-litre Perkins P6(V), mounted vertically at the front, with forward control, an exposed radiator, a full-width cab, and full-height bulkhead. The main frame, of 8½ in. × 2¾ in. section with six cross members, was straight except for a slight wheelarch, and was 26¾ in. high when laden. The whole chassis was straightforward and robust, without any unusual features. A standard 32-seat rear-entrance body was also made by Seddon if required, though bodies could be supplied by other firms too. Most Seddon buses in the first few years were exported, mostly for town services in places with similar conditions to Great Britain, and large fleets went to Bombay and Bermuda.

The "Mark 6" chassis appeared in September 1950. It was the same as Mark 4 except for a 16 ft. 4 in. wheelbase and 26 ft. overall length to carry up to 36 seats. By 1956 there was also a "Mark 6XR", the same as the other two except for the larger Perkins R6(V) engine and a 17 ft. 10 in. wheelbase for up to 30 ft. overall. The Mark 4 and Mark 6 were made continuously until 1963. They sold very well overseas, also to many independent operators in all parts of Britain, but very few to large companies or municipalities.

The somewhat smaller "Mark 7P" chassis, which was introduced in 1952, had the 3.15-litre Perkins P4(V) oil engine and an 11 ft. 8 in. wheelbase. With full-forward control, a very flat front, no separate bulkhead, and two seats alongside the driver, it was possible to get 28 seats for bus work in only 22 ft. overall length. But seat width was very cramped, as the vehicle was only 6 ft. 7 in. wide, and only really intended for places with very narrow roads and lots of sharp corners. Seddon's own bodywork was available if required. The Mark 7P remained on the market until 1963. By 1958 there was also a "Mark 7PX", with 13 ft. 4 in. wheelbase but otherwise the same.

Once firmly established with conventional types, Seddon introduced something dramatically new in September 1952. This was an underfloor-engined bus in which the engine was vertical and not horizontal. A standard Perkins was used, unaltered except for air cleaner and sump, located amidships under the central gangway, and projecting just a little above the top of the main frame. The frame height was straight and constant for the whole length of the bus, 35 in. laden and 38 in. unladen, and the floor level was 6 in. above this. The Seddon sold in three versions: "Mark 10P" with 13 ft. 11 in. wheelbase and Perkins P6(V) engine; "Mark 10R" with the same wheelbase but R6(V) engine; and "Mark 11" with 16 ft. 6 in. wheelbase and R6(V) engine. Overall lengths were 26 ft. and 30 ft., for up to 35 and 41 seats.

The other mechanical units of Marks 10 and 11 were similar to Marks 4 and 6, though their relative positions, and gear ratios, were different. The radiator was behind the front axle, and without any grille in the front panelling. The first Mark 10P was sold to the West Riding fleet at Wakefield. An Easy-Access trap for standing room when servicing the engine was provided by a detachable section of floor outside of the chassis frame on the near-side, so that a mechanic could stand on the garage floor with his waist through the bus floor.

Marks 10 and 11 ceased production in 1959. The Mark 17, which was introduced at the end of 1957, had either the P6 or the R6 engine mounted vertically at the front in a conventional layout, with 17 ft. 10 in. wheelbase for 33 ft. overall length. A Mark 18 with rear engine (the P6) also appeared in 1957, and a Mark 19 with horizontal underfloor-engine (the A.E.C. AH 410) came in 1959; both of these had 16 ft. 4 in. wheelbase. These three models later gave way to others that are still made today, and Seddon's psv bodywork has been extensively developed under the "Pennine" name

The Seddon Mark 4 chassis of 1948-63, with Perkins engine, is seen here in 1949 in the ownership of Oliver Taylor (Coaches) Ltd of Caterham, Surrey, on Epsom Downs on Derby Day.

This Seddon Mark 11 underfloor-engined coach with Duple body was originally used for the private transport of Ted Heath's Band from 1954, and 1 BMH was for Band Master Heath. In about 1960 it was sold to South Bedfordshire Coaches, of Clifton, Beds, and licensed as a psv.

# SENTINEL

*(Shrewsbury, Shropshire)*

Following the success of their underfloor-engined lorries Sentinel decided to enter the psv market with an underfloor-engined bus, at a time when these were still a very rare type, only B.M.M.O. and Leyland having yet made any. A prototype chassis was made in 1948, and tested. Sentinel then had to decide what type of bodywork to use. After trying many of the orthodox types they decided that the integrally-constructed bus was best for comfort and economy. So they teamed up with John C. Beadle Ltd of Dartford, Kent, who had already carried out many years of research in their chassisless under-structure. Sentinel acquired the right to make this and to use it in their own range of buses and coaches.

The Sentinel chassisless bus, known initially as the "Sentinel-Beadle", was an underfloor horizontal-engined 40-seater, built under the Beadle patents. The underframe comprised both the chassis and the body floor all in one unit, with two steel central longitudinal members, but with light alloy for the outer members and all the rest. Light alloy was also used for the whole of the body, to give a great saving in weight. The engine, mounted just behind the driver, was Sentinel's own 6.08-litre "4SRH2" four-cylinder oiler. The radiator and cooling fan were in the conventional position at the front of the bus, and thus remote from the engine. The wheelbase was 14 ft. 9 in., and the overall length and width 27 ft. 6 in. × 7 ft. 6 in. Sentinel advertised it as "the first British passenger bus to incorporate successfully the two most important improvements in design made during the past twenty years – the horizontal underfloor engine and the integral form of construction".

In September 1950 an enlarged 44-seat version was introduced. It had 15 ft. 7 in. wheelbase and 30 ft. × 8 ft. overall dimensions, and incorporated a new 9.12-litre six-cylinder "6SRH2" engine of the same bore and stroke. Both models were also available with fewer seats, spaced out wider. The official type designations were "STC 4/40" and "SLC 4/35" (four-cylinder short-wheelbase), and "STC 6/44" and "SLC 6/39" (six-cylinder long-wheelbase), the last figure indicating the number of seats. There was also an export model with 18 ft. 4 in. wheelbase, 33 ft. × 8 ft., using the 9.12 engine. Both engines were replaced in summer 1952 by new units with the same bore and stroke but direct injection instead of indirect, thus improving fuel economy and giving easier starting from cold.

Three new chassis with a conventional separate frame were also introduced in summer 1952. They had separate bodies built by other firms, notably Plaxton, Whitson, and Burlingham. The frame was perfectly straight, both in plan and in elevation, and had the same three wheelbases of 14 ft. 9 in., 15 ft. 7 in., and 18 ft. 4 in. to accommodate 8 ft. bodies of the same three lengths. These three chassis were known as types "STC 4/27", "STC 6/30", and "STC 6/33", and had direct-injection engines, 6.08 litres for the shorter chassis and 9.12 for the other two, all horizontally underfloor amidships. The radiator was still right at the front, but a lot lower down. For luxury coach work, as distinct from service buses, there was by 1953 also an "SLC 6/30" chassis, 30 ft. long, in which the spare wheel was mounted at the front, for a central entrance, instead of at the rear for a front entrance.

The 27 ft. chassis ceased to be made from 1954, and the other two from 1956. This ended all Sentinel bus and coach production, though lorries continued for a few more years. About 88 integral buses and coaches had been made for home use, plus 36 orthodox chassis Sentinels; only 11 were exported. At Carlisle and Penrith, Ribble Motor Services had 20 (six 40-seaters and 14 44-seaters), but all the rest were owned in ones and twos by small independents in rural areas throughout Britain.

The Sentinel factory was purchased by Rolls Royce Ltd in 1956, and is now used for the manufacture of their oil engines and Sentinel shunting locomotives.

The Sentinel STC 4/40 chassisless underfloor-engined vehicle of 1948-54, with Beadle bodywork, is seen in 1958 in the ownership of H. Nickolls & Son, of Milford, near Stafford, standing at the Stafford bus terminus.

The longer and wider Sentinel STC 6/44 of 1950-54, with a larger Sentinel engine and Beadle bodywork of improved frontal appearance, is standing in 1959 in the bus station at Penrith, Cumberland, in the fleet of Ribble Motor Services Ltd.

Sentinel also made coaches in 1952-4 with a separate chassis instead of integral bodywork. Here in 1961 is the underfloor-engined SLC 6/30 with Burlingham body, owned by A. Best & Sons, of Wembley, Middlesex.

# THORNYCROFT

*(Basingstoke, Hampshire)*

In 1947 a half-hearted attempt was made to return to the bus market by the re-appearance of the pre-war "Nippy" and "Sturdy" chassis. The Nippy had a 12 ft. 6 in. wheelbase for 20 seats and forward control, with a four-cylinder petrol engine; and the Sturdy had a 17 ft. 6 in. wheelbase for 26 seats and normal control with a six-cylinder oil engine. Both were a lengthened goods chassis, and not many were sold in bus form despite the widespread success of Thornycroft buses before the war, and they vanished again in 1950. The pre-war double-deckers and larger single-deckers did not appear at all after the war, though a large fleet of heavy-duty long-distance six-wheel buses with 150 bhp petrol engines was sold to the South African Railways. The "Trident" of 1957 was a 12 ton lorry chassis with 5½-litre oil engine, but a few were used as buses in some of the more remote foreign countries.

The Thornycroft Nippy was a popular 1938-9 chassis of which a few more were sold in 1947-50. This one, with Waveney bodywork, was owned by Tillingbourne Valley Services Ltd of Chilworth, near Guildford, Surrey, and was seen in 1954 at Guildford bus station.

# TILLING-STEVENS

*(Maidstone, Kent)*

In 1937 Tilling-Stevens was the first firm to make an underfloor-engined bus, and they were the only people ever to do it with eight cylinders or with six wheels. Unfortunately they made only the prototype, and never sold any, and it nearly bankrupted them. After the war they tried again, with a new but orthodox design, of which a fair number were sold. The “K6LA7” and “K5LA7” were announced in May 1946, but the first one did not appear until November 1947, although a few had earlier gone to Hong Kong. These two chassis had, respectively, the 6LW Gardner engine for fast 32-seat coaches, and the 5LW Gardner for slower 36-seat buses. Their wheelbases were 17 ft. 3 in. for 27 ft. 6 in. overall length, and they had a plain conventional main frame. The only unusual feature was the use of the bulkhead structure to support the rear end of the engine. An exposed and very large radiator was used, with half-cab layout. The “K6MA7” chassis appeared in September 1948. This was the same as above, except for a Meadows 6DC.630 engine.

Also in September 1948 they introduced a new “L6PA7” chassis, using the well-tried Perkins P6(V) engine in a new and lightweight frame. This model had a 17 ft. 6 in. wheelbase for 27 ft. 6 in. overall length and seated 32. After two years the L6PA7 was dropped, and replaced by a “L4MA8” or “Express Mark II” chassis. This also was a lightweight vehicle, with straight high frame, and 18 ft. 7½ in. wheelbase for 30 ft. overall length. Instead of the Perkins it used the new four-cylinder Meadows 4DC.330 oil engine. On 4 September 1950 the company was purchased by Rootes Ltd which already owned Commer (and others). The three heavy models were dropped in 1951, and the lightweight L4MA8 in 1952. No more chassis were made after this, and the Maidstone factory was turned over to making the new Rootes TS3 two-stroke engine for fitting into Commer chassis.

The Tilling-Stevens K6LA7 and K6MA7 of 1947-51, with Gardner and Meadows engine, both had the same frontal appearance. Here in 1957 is one with Vincent bodywork, owned by Chiltern Queens Ltd of Woodcote, Oxfordshire.

The Tilling-Stevens L4MA8 or Express Mark II, of 1950-52, was the last chassis made by T.S.M. before closing down. This one was owned by R. Parkhouse & Sons, of Penclawdd, Glamorganshire, and is seen in 1952 in Swansea.

# TROJAN

*(Croydon, Surrey)*

From 1954 to 1962 Trojan made a small 12-seater with forward control and a 9 ft. 4 in. wheelbase. It was 6 ft. 6 in. wide, about 16 ft. long, and the engine was the Perkins P3(V). This was an unusual three-cylinder unit, in effect only one half of the more common P6(V), with the same pistons and cylinders but a different crankshaft. From 1958 the engine was changed to the new Perkins "Four 99" diesel, with four cylinders of 99 cu. in. capacity. Two standard bodies, a bus or a coach, were offered, and many were operated by small independents in remote rural areas in various parts of Britain.

The Trojan 12-seater was made in 1952-64, and this one was bought by House Bros, of Watlington, Oxfordshire, where we see it in 1966.

# VULCAN

*(Maidstone, Kent)*

Vulcan started in 1897 at Southport in Lancashire, building private cars and later lorries and buses, including double-deckers from 1931. The company was purchased in 1937 by Tilling-Stevens Ltd, of Maidstone, Kent whereupon bus and coach making ceased for 12 years, and the making of van and lorry chassis was transferred from Southport to Maidstone. At the end of 1949 Vulcan produced a medium-sized single-deck chassis with a 15 ft. 3 in. wheelbase suitable for 26 ft. bodywork. It had forward-control layout, a full-width cab, and a Perkins P6(V) oil engine. Many small independent operators bought it, but production ceased after only a year or two after Vulcan had been purchased by Rootes Ltd, in 1950.

Vulcan was a famous name for many years before the war, but afterwards the only buses or coaches they sold were a few of this type in 1949-51. This one, owned by Safeguard Coaches Ltd of Guildford, Surrey, had a Dutfield body, and was seen in 1951.

# ENGINES FOR BRITISH BUSES MADE BETWEEN 1945 AND 1965

For cylinder dimensions some manufacturers have always used inches and others have always used millimetres, so they are quoted here in the form used by the makers. Many firms, however, have always quoted cubic capacity both in cubic inches and in litres or cubic centimetres, and the few that did not have been converted to the other form for the purposes of this table so as to afford a basis for direct comparison of engine sizes.

| *Engine make and model* | *Chassis in which used* | *Petrol or oil* | *Vertical or horizontal* | *Number of cylinders, bore and stroke* | | *Cubic capacity* | | *Compression ratio, to 1* | *R.A.C. hp rating* | *Maximum bhp at rpm* | *Maximum torque, lb.-ft. at rpm* | *Years of manufacture (very approx.)* |
|---|---|---|---|---|---|---|---|---|---|---|---|---|
| | | | | *in.* | *mm.* | *cu.in.* | *litres* | | | | | |
| A.E.C. 7.7 litre | 661, 662, 681, 682, K6A, CWA6, Maudslay | O | V | | 6; 105 × 146 | 462 | 7.58 | 16 | 41.0 | 108 at 2000 | 325 at 1100 | 1934-54 |
| A.E.C. 9.6 litre | 961, 962, 3RT | O | V | | 6; 120 × 142 | 588 | 9.64 | 16 | 53.7 | 125 at 1800 | 430 at 1000 | 1939-58 |
| A.E.C. 9.6 litre | Regal 4 | O | H | | 6; 120 × 142 | 588 | 9.64 | 16 | 53.7 | 125 at 1800 | 430 at 1000 | 1950-58 |
| A.E.C. 11.3 litre | Regal 5 | O | V | | 6; 130 × 142 | 690 | 11.31 | 16 | 62.9 | 153 at 1800 | 505 at 1100 | 1950-58 |
| A.E.C. 11.3 litre | Regal 6 | O | H | | 6; 130 × 142 | 690 | 11.31 | 16 | 62.9 | 153 at 1800 | 505 at 1100 | 1950-58 |
| A.E.C. AV 410 | | O | V | | 6; 105 × 130 | 410 | 6.75 | 16 | 41.0 | 98 at 2000 | 282 at 1300 | 1954- |
| A.E.C. AH 410 | Reliance, Monocoach, Rowe | O | H | | 6; 105 × 130 | 410 | 6.75 | 16 | 41.0 | 98 at 2000 | 282 at 1300 | 1953- |
| A.E.C. AV 470 | Regent V, Ranger | O | V | | 6; 112 × 130 | 470 | 7.68 | 16 | 46.6 | 112 at 2000 | 325 at 1100 | 1954- |
| A.E.C. AH 470 | Reliance, Rowe | O | H | | 6; 112 × 130 | 470 | 7.68 | 16 | 46.6 | 112 at 2000 | 325 at 1100 | 1953- |
| A.E.C. AV 590 | Regent V, Bridgemaster, Renown, RM | O | V | | 6; 120 × 142 | 588 | 9.64 | 16 | 53.7 | 125 at 1800 | 430 at 1000 | 1958- |
| A.E.C. AH 590 | Reliance | O | H | | 6; 120 × 142 | 588 | 9.64 | 16 | 53.7 | 125 at 1800 | 430 at 1000 | 1958- |
| A.E.C. AV 690 | | O | V | | 6; 130 × 142 | 690 | 11.31 | 16 | 62.9 | 150 at 1800 | 505 at 1100 | 1958- |
| A.E.C. AH 690 | Regal 6 | O | H | | 6; 130 × 142 | 690 | 11.31 | 16 | 62.9 | 150 at 1800 | 505 at 1100 | 1958- |
| Albion | Valkyrie CX9 | P | V | $4; 4\tfrac{5}{8} \times 5\tfrac{1}{2}$ | | 370 | 6.06 | | 34.2 | 85 at 2200 | | 1933-48 |
| Albion 52/120 | Valkyrie CX13 | P | V | $6; 4\tfrac{5}{8} \times 5\tfrac{1}{2}$ | | 555 | 9.09 | | 51.3 | 120 at 2200 | | 1937-48 |
| Albion 52/105 | Valkyrie CX13, Venturer CX19 | O | V | $6; 4\tfrac{5}{8} \times 5\tfrac{1}{2}$ | | 555 | 9.09 | | 51.3 | 105 at 1800 | | 1938-48 |
| Albion | Valkyrie CX9 | O | V | $4; 4\tfrac{5}{8} \times 6$ | | 403 | 6.61 | | 34.2 | 78 at 1800 | | 1945-50 |
| Albion EN 253 | Venturer CX37, Viking CX41, Viking HD61 | O | V | $6; 4\tfrac{5}{8} \times 6$ | | 604 | 9.92 | | 51.3 | 120 at 1700 | 413 at 1000 | 1947-64 |
| Albion | Victor FT3AB | P | V | $6; 3\tfrac{1}{2} \times 4\tfrac{1}{2}$ | | 260 | 4.26 | | 29.4 | 80 at 2800 | | 1945-52 |
| Albion EN 286 | Victor FT39 | O | V | $4; 4\tfrac{1}{4} \times 5\tfrac{1}{4}$ | | 298 | 4.88 | | 28.9 | 75 at 2000 | 208 at 1200 | 1945-56 |
| Albion EN 287 | Victor FT39KA | O | V | $4; 4\tfrac{1}{2} \times 5\tfrac{1}{4}$ | | 334 | 5.58 | | 32.4 | 81 at 2000 | 233 at 1200 | 1956-59 |
| Albion EN 289 | Victor VT13 | O | V | $4; 4\tfrac{1}{2} \times 5\tfrac{1}{4}$ | | 334 | 5.58 | 14.5 | 32.4 | 94 at 2200 | 252 at 1250 | 1959-64 |
| Albion EN 219 | Nimbus MR9 | O | H | $4; 4 \times 4\tfrac{3}{4}$ | | 234 | 3.83 | | 25.6 | 60 at 2200 | 160 at 1200 | 1956-58 |
| Albion EN 250 | Nimbus NS3N | O | H | $4; 4\tfrac{1}{8} \times 4\tfrac{3}{4}$ | | 250 | 410 | 16 | 27.2 | 72 at 2200 | 190 at 1300 | 1958-64 |
| Austin | CXB | P | V | $6; 3\tfrac{3}{8} \times 4$ | | 211 | 3.46 | | 27.3 | 67 at 2900 | | 1939-49 |
| Austin 3.99 litre | Coach | P | V | $6; 3\tfrac{7}{16} \times 4\tfrac{3}{8}$ | | 244 | 3.99 | 6.15 | 28.4 | 68 at 2700 | 174 at 1000 | 1949-56 |
| Austin 3.99 litre | Series III | P | V | $6; 3\tfrac{7}{16} \times 4\tfrac{3}{8}$ | | 244 | 3.99 | 6.4 | 28.4 | 87 at 3000 | 196 at 1000 | 1956- |
| B.M.C. 5.10 litre | Series III, Guy Warrior, Guy Otter | O | V | | 6; 95 × 120 | 311 | 5.10 | 16.5 | 33.6 | 90 at 2400 | 228 at 1500 | 1956- |

| Engine make and model | Chassis in which used | Petrol or oil | Vertical or horizontal | Number of cylinders, bore and stroke | | Cubic capacity | | Compression ratio, to 1 | R.A.C. hp rating | Maximum bhp at rpm | Maximum torque, lb.-ft. at rpm | Years of manufacture (very approx.) |
|---|---|---|---|---|---|---|---|---|---|---|---|---|
| | | | | in. | mm. | cu.in. | litres | | | | | |
| B.M.M.O 8 litre | D5 | O | V | 6; 4 7/16 × 5 1/4 | | 488 | 8.0 | 16 | 47.2 | | | 1936-55 |
| B.M.M.O 8 litre | S6, S7, S8, S9, S10, S11, S12 | O | H | 6; 4 7/16 × 5 1/4 | | 488 | 8.0 | 16 | 47.2 | 98 at 1700 | 345 at 1000 | 1946-52 |
| B.M.M.O 10½ litre | S13 | O | H | | 6; 124 × 145 | 640 | 10.5 | 16 | 57.2 | 125 at 1700 | 466 at 800 | 1950-60 |
| Bedford 214 cu. in. | OWB, OB | P | V | 6; 3 3/8 × 4 | | 214 | 3.52 | 6.2 | 27.3 | 72 at 3000 | 161 at 1200 | 1938-50 |
| Bedford 214 cu. in. | J2SZ2 | P | V | 6; 3 3/8 × 4 | | 214 | 3.52 | 6.2 | 27.3 | 86 at 3400 | 170 at 1200 | 1950 |
| Bedford 214 cu. in. | C4Z1, VAS2 | P | V | 6; 3 3/8 × 4 | | 214 | 3.52 | 6.2 | 27.3 | 100 at 3600 | 184 at 1200 | 1957 |
| Bedford 300 cu. in. | SB | P | V | 6; 3 7/8 × 4 1/4 | | 300 | 4.93 | 6.0 | 36.0 | 110 at 3200 | 234 at 1200 | 1950-54 |
| Bedford 300 cu. in. | SB | P | V | 6; 3 7/8 × 4 1/4 | | 300 | 4.93 | 6.5 | 36.0 | 115 at 3200 | 236 at 1400 | 1954-60 |
| Bedford 300 cu. in. | SB3 | P | V | 6; 3 7/8 × 4 1/4 | | 300 | 4.93 | 6.6 | 36.0 | 133 at 3400 | 267 at 1200 | 1960- |
| Bedford 300 cu. in. | SB1, C4Z2, VAS1 | O | V | 6; 3 7/8 × 4 1/4 | | 300 | 4.93 | 17 | 36.0 | 97 at 2800 | 217 at 1400 | 1960- |
| Bedford 330 cu. in. | SB5, VAS5 | O | V | 6; 4 1/16 × 4 1/4 | | 330 | 5.42 | 17 | 39.6 | 105 at 3000 | 255 at 1400 | 1962 |
| Bedford 220 cu. in. | J2SZ10 | O | V | 4; 4 1/16 × 4 1/4 | | 220 | 3.61 | 17 | 26.4 | 63 at 2600 | 153 at 1400 | 1962- |
| Bristol AVW | K6B, L6B, LD6B | O | V | | 6; 110 × 143 | 497 | 8.15 | | 45.0 | 100 at 1700 | 337 at 1200 | 1948-58 |
| Bristol AVW | LS6B, MW6B | O | H | | 6; 110 × 143 | 497 | 8.15 | | 45.0 | 100 at 1700 | 337 at 1200 | 1953-65 |
| Bristol BVW | LD6B, FLF6B | O | H | | 6; 115 × 143 | 543 | 8.90 | 16.1 | 49.2 | 105 at 1600 | 380 at 1150 | 1958-65 |
| Commer 16 hp | Karrier | P | V | | 4; 81 × 110 | 138 | 2.27 | 6.25 | 16.3 | 56 at 3400 | 104 at 1600 | 1939- |
| Commer 27 hp | Commando | P | V | | 6; 85 × 120 | 249 | 4.08 | | 26.9 | 80 at 3100 | 178 at 1200 | 1936-52 |
| Commer QX | Avenger, Beadle, Harrington | P | 66° | 6; 3 3/4 × 4 3/8 | | 290 | 4.75 | 6.15 | 33.8 | 109 at 3000 | 230 at 1200 | 1948- |
| Rootes TS3 2-stroke | Avenger, Beadle, Harrington | O | H | 3; 3 1/4 × 4 | | 199 | 3.26 | 16 | 12.6 | 105 at 2400 | 270 at 1200 | 1954- |
| Crossley 8.6 litre | DD42, SD42 | O | V | 6; 4 1/2 × 5 1/2 | | 525 | 8.59 | 15.6 | 48.6 | 100 at 1750 | 377 at 1000 | 1945-50 |
| Cummins V6 | Daimler Roadliner | O | V | 6; 5 1/2 × 4 1/8 | | 588 | 9.63 | 16.9 | 72.6 | 150 at 2100 | 405 at 1200 | 1964- |
| Daimler CD6 | CWD6, CVD6, CLD6 | O | V | 6; 4 1/2 × 5 1/2 | | 525 | 8.60 | 15 | 48.6 | 100 at 1800 | 350 at 1200 | 1945-65 |
| Daimler CDS6 | Turbocharged CVD6-SD | O | V | 6; 4 1/2 × 5 1/2 | | 525 | 8.60 | 15 | 48.6 | 148 at 2000 | 460 at 1250 | 1958-65 |
| Daimler CD650 | CVD650 | O | V | 6; 5 × 5 1/2 | | 650 | 10.62 | 15 | 60.0 | 150 at 2000 | 460 at 850 | 1948-65 |
| Daimler CD650H | Freeline Home | O | H | 6; 5 × 5 1/2 | | 650 | 10.62 | 15 | 60.0 | 125 at 1800 | 460 at 850 | 1951-65 |
| Daimler CD650H | Freeline Export | O | H | 6; 5 × 5 1/2 | | 650 | 10.62 | 15 | 60.0 | 150 at 2000 | 460 at 850 | 1954-65 |
| Dennis petrol | Falcon | P | V | | 4; 100 × 120 | 230 | 3.77 | | 24.8 | 75 at 3000 | | 1933-50 |
| Dennis 5 litre | Falcon | O | V | | 6; 98 × 112 | 308 | 5.06 | | 35.7 | 75 at 2000 | 220 at 1000 | 1950-54 |
| Dennis 5½ litre | Falcon | O | V | | 6; 102 × 112 | 335 | 5.50 | 15 3/4 | 38.7 | 87 at 2000 | 240 at 1100 | 1952-57 |
| Dennis 5½ litre | Pelican | O | H | | 6; 102 × 112 | 335 | 5.50 | 15 3/4 | 39.5 | 92 at 2200 | 242 at 1200 | 1954-57 |
| Dennis O6 | Lancet J3, J10, Lance K3 | O | V | | 6; 105 × 146 | 462 | 7.58 | 15 | 41.0 | 100 at 1800 | 335 at 1000 | 1945-62 |
| Dennis O6 | Dominant, Lancet UF | O | H | | 6; 105 × 146 | 462 | 7.58 | 15 | 41.0 | 110 at 2000 | 328 at 1250 | 1954-62 |
| Dennis 8 litre | Loline | O | V | | 6; 108 × 146 | 490 | 8.03 | 15.6 | 43.4 | 120 at 1800 | 368 at 1100 | 1958- |
| Foden FD6 two-stroke | PVDE6, PVFE6, PVRF6 | O | V | | 6; 85 × 120 | 250 | 4.09 | 14 | 26.9 | 126 at 2000 | 350 at 1500 | 1948-56 |

| Engine make and model | Chassis in which used | Petrol or oil | Vertical or horizontal | Number of cylinders, bore and stroke: in. | Number of cylinders, bore and stroke: mm. | Cubic capacity: cu.in. | Cubic capacity: litres | Compression ratio, to 1 | R.A.C. hp rating | Maximum bhp at rpm | Maximum torque, lb.-ft. at rpm | Years of manufacture (very approx.) |
|---|---|---|---|---|---|---|---|---|---|---|---|---|
| Ford petrol | Thames P.S.V. | P | V | | 6; 95 × 115 | 298 | 4.89 | 6.4 | 33.6 | 109 at 3000 | 242 at 1500 | ? |
| Ford 6D oil | Thames P.S.V. | O | V | | 6; 100 × 115 | 330 | 5.42 | 16 | 37.2 | 100 at 2500 | 242 at 1500 | ? |
| Gardner 4LK | Bristol SC, Dennis Falcon, Guy Otter | O | V | 4; $3\frac{3}{4} \times 5\frac{1}{4}$ | | 232 | 3.80 | | 22.5 | 57 at 2100 | 161 at 900 | 1938- |
| Gardner 4LW | Dennis Falcon, Guy Warrior | O | V | 4; $4\frac{1}{4} \times 6$ | | 340 | 5.58 | 13 | 28.9 | 75 at 1700 | 237 at 1300 | 1931- |
| Gardner 5LW | K5G, L5G, CVG5, CLG5, Arab, Foden, LD5G | O | V | 5; $4\frac{1}{4} \times 6$ | | 426 | 6.97 | 13 | 36.1 | 94 at 1700 | 300 at 1300 | 1931- |
| Gardner 6LW | K6G, L6G, LD6G, CVG6, Arab, Foden, T.S.M. | O | V | 6; $4\frac{1}{4} \times 6$ | | 511 | 8.37 | 13 | 43.3 | 112 at 1700 | 358 at 1300 | 1931- |
| Gardner 4HLW | LS4G, Alpha, Rowe | O | H | 4; $4\frac{1}{4} \times 6$ | | 340 | 5.58 | 13 | 28.9 | 75 at 1700 | 237 at 1300 | 1950- |
| Gardner 5HLW | LS5G, MW5G, Alpha, Arab, Warrior, Rowe | O | H | 5; $4\frac{1}{4} \times 6$ | | 426 | 6.97 | 13 | 36.1 | 94 at 1700 | 300 at 1300 | 1950- |
| Gardner 6HLW | LS6G, MW6G, Alpha, Arab, Freeline | O | H | 6; $4\frac{1}{4} \times 6$ | | 511 | 8.37 | 13 | 43.3 | 112 at 1700 | 358 at 1300 | 1950- |
| Gardner 6LX | CVG6, Fleetline, Loline, Wulfrunian | O | V | 6; $4\frac{3}{4} \times 6$ | | 638 | 10.45 | 14 | 54.2 | 150 at 1700 | 485 at 1000 | 1958- |
| Gardner 6HLX | Freeline | O | H | 6; $4\frac{3}{4} \times 6$ | | 638 | 10.45 | 14 | 54.2 | 150 at 1700 | 485 at 1000 | 1965- |
| Guy 50 hp | Wolf | P | V | | 4; 90 × 130 | 202 | 3.31 | | 20.1 | 50 at 2400 | 140 at 1400 | 1933-55 |
| Guy 60 hp | Vixen, Otter | P | V | | 4; 95 × 130 | 225 | 3.69 | | 22.4 | 60 at 2400 | 165 at 1400 | 1936-55 |
| Leyland 7.4 litre | Titan PD1, Tiger PS1 | O | V | 6; $4\frac{3}{8} \times 5$ | | 451 | 7.39 | | 45.9 | 100 at 1800 | 328 at 1150 | 1945-48 |
| Leyland petrol | Comet | P | V | 6; $3.80 \times 4\frac{1}{2}$ | | 306 | 5.02 | 6 | 34.7 | 100 at 2400 | 232 at 1200 | 1946-51 |
| Leyland 0.300 | Comet | O | V | 6; $3.80 \times 4\frac{1}{2}$ | | 306 | 5.02 | 16 | 34.7 | 75 at 2000 | 220 at 1000 | 1947-53 |
| Leyland 0.350 | Comet 90, Bedford SB8 | O | V | 6; $3.96 \times 4\frac{3}{4}$ | | 351 | 5.76 | 16 | 37.6 | 90 at 2200 | 240 at 1300 | 1953-62 |
| Leyland 0.350 | Tiger Cub Bus | O | H | 6; $3.96 \times 4\frac{3}{4}$ | | 351 | 5.76 | 16 | 37.6 | 90 at 2200 | 240 at 1300 | 1952-62 |
| Leyland 0.350 | Olympian, Aberdonian | O | H | 6; $3.96 \times 4\frac{3}{4}$ | | 351 | 5.76 | 16 | 37.6 | 94 at 2000 | 255 at 1400 | 1957- |
| Leyland 0.350 | Tiger Cub Coach, Dodge 3090Y | O | H | 6; $3.96 \times 4\frac{3}{4}$ | | 351 | 5.76 | 16 | 37.6 | 108 at 2400 | 257 at 1500 | 1952- |
| Leyland 0.370 | Comet 90, Victor VT17, Dodge KS700 | O | V | 6; $4.07 \times 4\frac{3}{4}$ | | 371 | 6.07 | 16 | 39.8 | 115 at 2400 | 272 at 1600 | 1962- |
| Leyland 0.400 | Comet export, Bedford VAL | O | V | 6; $4.22 \times 4\frac{3}{4}$ | | 399 | 6.54 | 16 | 42.8 | 131 at 2400 | 300 at 1600 | 1963- |
| Leyland 0.400 | Panther Cub, Tiger Cub | O | H | 6; $4.22 \times 4\frac{3}{4}$ | | 399 | 6.54 | 16 | 42.8 | 131 at 2400 | 300 at 1600 | 1962- |
| Leyland 0.600 | PD2 ,PD3, PS2, Atlantean, Lowlander, Wulfrunian | O | V | 6; $4.80 \times 5\frac{1}{2}$ | | 597 | 9.78 | 15.7 | 55.3 | 125 at 1800 | 410 at 900 | 1947- |
| Leyland 0.600 | Royal Tiger, Olympic, Leopard bus, Panther | O | H | 6; $4.80 \times 5\frac{1}{2}$ | | 597 | 9.78 | 15.7 | 55.3 | 125 at 1800 | 410 at 900 | 1948- |
| Leyland 0.600 | Leopard Coach, Panther Coach | O | H | 6; $4.80 \times 5\frac{1}{2}$ | | 597 | 9.78 | 15.7 | 55.3 | 130 at 2200 | 405 at 1400 | 1960- |
| Leyland 0.680 | Atlantean | O | V | 6; $5.00 \times 5\frac{3}{4}$ | | 677 | 11.1 | 15.8 | 60.0 | 153 at 1750 | 446 at 1000 | 1958- |
| Leyland 0.680 | Worldmaster, Guy Victory | O | H | 6; $5.00 \times 5\frac{3}{4}$ | | 677 | 11.1 | 15.8 | 60.0 | 155 at 2000 | 470 at 1100 | 1954- |

| Engine make and model | Chassis in which used | Petrol or oil | Vertical or horizontal | Number of cylinders, bore and stroke: in. | Number of cylinders, bore and stroke: mm. | Cubic capacity: cu.in. | Cubic capacity: litres | Compression ratio, to 1 | R.A.C. hp rating | Maximum bhp at rpm | Maximum torque, lb.-ft. at rpm | Years of manufacture (very approx.) |
|---|---|---|---|---|---|---|---|---|---|---|---|---|
| Maudslay | Marathon | P | V | | 6; 110 × 130 | 452 | 7.41 | | 45.0 | 100 at 1700 | | 1946-49 |
| Meadows 4DC.330 | Guy Warrior, Rowe, Rutland, T.S.M. | O | V | 4; 4¾ × 4¾ | | 331 | 5.43 | 16 | 35.7 | 98 at 2400 | 240 at 1400 | 1950- |
| Meadows 4HDC.330 | Guy Warrior, Rowe, Rutland | O | H | 4; 4¾ × 4¾ | | 331 | 5.43 | 16 | 35.7 | 85 at 2200 | 230 at 1300 | 1956- |
| Meadows 6DC.500 | | O | V | 6; 4¾ × 4¾ | | 497 | 8.14 | 16 | 54.2 | 150 at 2400 | 358 at 1500 | ? |
| Meadows 6HDC.500 | Guy Victory, Rowe | O | H | 6; 4¾ × 4¾ | | 497 | 8.14 | 16 | 54.2 | 150 at 2600 | 346 at 1450 | ? |
| Meadows 6DC.630 | Guy Arab, T.S.M. | O | V | 6; 5⅛ × 5⅛ | | 633 | 10.35 | 16 | 63.0 | 130 at 1900 | 415 at 900 | 1946- |
| Meadows 6HDC.630 | Guy Arab U/F | O | H | 6; 5⅛ × 5⅛ | | 633 | 10.35 | 16 | 63.0 | 143 at 1900 | 428 at 1200 | 1955- |
| Morris-Commercial | (petrol) PP | P | V | | 4; 100 × 120 | 230 | 3.77 | | 24.8 | 80 at 3000 | 179 at 1750 | 1949-55 |
| Morris-Commercial | (Saurer) OP | O | V | | 6; 85 × 125 | 259 | 4.25 | 19 | 26.9 | 75 at 2400 | 167 at 1500 | 1948-50 |
| Morris-Commercial | (Saurer) OP | O | V | | 6; 87 × 125 | 273 | 4.47 | 19 | 28.2 | 70 at 2400 | | 1950- |
| Perkins P3(V) | Trojan | O | V | 3; 3½ × 5 | | 144 | 2.36 | | 14.7 | 41 at 2400 | 101 at 1400 | 1952- |
| Perkins P4(V) | Seddon Mk 7 | O | V | 4; 3½ × 5 | | 192 | 3.15 | | 19.6 | 46 at 2200 | 123 at 1400 | 1946-61 |
| Perkins P4(V) | conversions from petrol | O | V | 4; 3½ × 5 | | 192 | 3.15 | | 19.6 | 54 at 2400 | 133 at 1500 | 1946-61 |
| Perkins P6(V) | Beadle, Jensen, Tilling-Stevens, Vulcan | O | V | 6; 3½ × 5 | | 289 | 4.73 | 16.5 | 29.4 | 70 at 2200 | 184 at 1300 | 1946-61 |
| Perkins P6(V) | Seddon Mk 4, Mk 6, Mk 10P, Dodge 86 & 87 | O | V | 6; 3½ × 5 | | 289 | 4.73 | 16.5 | 29.4 | 83 at 2400 | 204 at 1500 | 1946-61 |
| Perkins R6(V) | Seddon 6XR, 10R, 11, Rutland, Bedford SBO | O | V | 6; 4 × 4½ | | 339 | 5.56 | 17.5 | 38.4 | 108 at 2700 | 240 at 1550 | 1954- |
| Perkins Four-99 | Trojan | O | V | 4; 3 × 3½ | | 99 | 1.60 | 20 | 18.0 | 42 at 3600 | 110 at 2200 | 1958- |
| Perkins Four-192 | conversions from petrol | O | V | 4; 3½ × 5 | | 192 | 3.15 | | 19.6 | 62 at 3000 | 143 at 1350 | 1961- |
| Perkins Four-203 | conversions from petrol | O | V | 4; 3⅝ × 5 | | 203 | 3.33 | | 20.4 | 63 at 2600 | 147 at 1350 | 1960- |
| Perkins Six-305 | Dodge 3087P | O | V | 6; 3⅝ × 5 | | 305 | 5.00 | 17.4 | 30.6 | 89 at 2600 | 218 at 1250 | 1960- |
| Perkins Four-236 | conversions from petrol | O | V | 4; 3⅞ × 5 | | 236 | 3.88 | 16 | 24.0 | 80 at 2800 | 193 at 1400 | 1964- |
| Perkins Six-354 | Dodge 3090T | O | V | 6; 3⅞ × 5 | | 354 | 5.80 | 16 | 36.0 | 112 at 2800 | 260 at 1450 | 1960- |
| Rolls-Royce B60-6P | Harrington Contender | P | V | 6; 3½ × 4½ | | 260 | 4.25 | 6.40 | 29.4 | 122 at 4000 | 215 at 2250 | ? |
| Rolls-Royce B80-8P | Harrington Contender | P | V | 8; 3½ × 4½ | | 346 | 5.67 | 6.40 | 39.2 | 160 at 4000 | 275 at 1750 | ? |
| Sentinel 4SRH2 Comet | STC4/40, SLC4/35 | O | H | 4; 4¾ × 5¼ | | 370 | 6.08 | | 36.1 | 90 at 2000 | 255 at 1500 | 1948-52 |
| Sentinel 6SRH2 Comet | STC6/44, SLC6/39 | O | H | 6; 4¾ × 5¼ | | 557 | 9.12 | | 54.2 | 135 at 2000 | | 1950-52 |
| Sentinel 4SRH2 d.i. | STC4/27 | O | H | 4; 4¾ × 5¼ | | 370 | 6.08 | 16¾ | 36.1 | 80 at 1800 | | 1952-58 |
| Sentinel 6SRH2 d.i. | STC6/30, STC6/33, SLC6/30 | O | H | 6; 4¾ × 5¼ | | 557 | 9.12 | 16¾ | 54.2 | 120 at 1800 | 375 at 1100 | 1952-58 |
| Standard | Karrier | O | V | 4; 3¼ × 4 | | 138 | 2.26 | | 16.9 | 54 at 3000 | 99 at 1850 | 1960- |
| Thornycroft ER4 | Nippy | P | V | 4; 3⅞ × 5 | | 235 | 3.86 | | 24.0 | 68 at 2600 | 163 at 1500 | 1937-? |
| Thornycroft TR6 | Sturdy | O | V | 6; 3⅝ × 4⅛ | | 253 | 4.14 | | 31.5 | 67 at 2200 | 174 at 1300 | 1939-? |